# RETIRE STRONG!

## YOUR GUIDE TO A HAPPY AND WORRY-FREE RETIREMENT

### ERIC T. SCOGGINS, CFP®

Printed in the United States of America

First Printing, 2016

Gradient Positioning Systems, LLC
4105 Lexington Avenue North, Suite 110
Arden Hills, MN 55126
(877) 901-0894

Contributors: Nick Stovall, Mike Binger, Nate Lucius and Gradient Positioning Systems, LLC.

# TABLE OF CONTENTS

# WELCOME TO THE RETIREMENT JOURNEY

*"Do all the good you can. By all the means you can. In all the ways you can. In all the places you can. At all the times you can. To all the people you can. As long as ever you can."*
*— John Wesley*

As you stand on the threshold of retirement, looking out at what you hope will be your golden years, you want to know that you are doing all the good you can to secure a happy outcome. Most people spend so much time getting TO retirement, they forget to think about how they will get THROUGH retirement. To that end, many worthwhile comparisons can be made between taking a trip of a lifetime and the time in your life called *retirement*. As with any journey, it's not just the destination that matters: it's about enjoying yourself along the way.

» *Gary and Marie have been planning their road trip to Florida for over a year now and they can't wait to get there. Gary has rented a resort condo with all the amenities on a private beach. They will relax in lounge chairs and sip on drinks with little paper umbrellas. They will swim in the ocean, stroll along the beach, stay up late and rent movies, sleep in and order room service. Marie has bought new beach attire for the trip; Gary has the address of their destination already entered into his GPS and has downloaded all of their favorite beach music to his phone. He also has an app called "Gas Buddy" that will always tell them where the closest gas station is to their location. It took forever for this day to come, but finally, it's here! Full of excitement and anticipation, Gary and Marie load up the car and back out of the driveway. After more than a year of hoping, dreaming, and planning, they are finally on the road!*

*At first things are great: Marie blasts the air conditioner and Gary blasts his favorite tunes. They see a few sights along the way and have a picnic lunch. Then just after noon on their first day, they hit their first bump in the road—major construction. They are re-routed into an unfamiliar area not recognized by their GPS. They get turned around, and because they didn't bring a paper map, the detour ends up costing them over an hour of time. They arrive late to the restaurant they planned to eat at that evening, only to discover that it recently went out of business. On cue, it starts to rain. It's really coming down along with great displays of lightning, and Gary misses their next exit. Tired, hungry, and worried about the storm, they drive 20 miles out of their way before they figure out how to get back on track.*

*When they get their bearings, it is well after ten o'clock and they are hours away from their hotel. They are driving on a long stretch of lonely highway when suddenly, the Low Fuel light comes on. Gary and Marie look at each other. They both get a bad feeling in the pit of their stomachs. Marie turns off the AC, Gary turns off the radio. He takes out his cell to access his Gas Buddy app, only to discover they are in a "No Service" zone.*

*"I think I saw a gas station a few miles back," says Marie. They do a U-turn and drive back there, but the gas station is closed. They are almost out of fuel, it's raining, and they are miles from their destination. Panic ensues. "Why didn't you bring a paper map?" Why did you tell me to turn around?" Why didn't you fill up at the last exit?" They are tense, and accusations fly back and forth. They say things to each other they maybe should not say, and as the night sky darkens and the rain continues to pour, their dream vacation slowly falls apart.*

Many people start out their retirement journey like Gary and Marie, happy and excited, but without a strong enough plan in place. You, like them, might have some idea of where you are going and a collection of investments you packed for the journey such as mutual fund portfolios, IRAs and 401(k)s. Do you know how all the pieces come together to get you to where you want to go? And what will you do when life throws those unexpected detours along the way? Running out of gas is not a fun thing to experience, but it pales in comparison the fear of running out of money during retirement.

**Many people today are making major mistakes when it comes to their retirement. They are suffering not because they didn't work hard or save and invest enough money, but because they are not receiving good, objective advice for the second half of the financial game of life.** This stage of the game is called *the distribution phase*, and far too many people are using strategies and tools that are simply antiquated and not as effective for today's unique financial times.

**Many Americans are living in a constant state of time poverty in an information-overloaded society. They are perplexed and confused about how to best protect their nest egg and generate income at a time in their lives when they need the money the most.**

There is also a tremendous void in our traditional educational system. No one is taught what to do with their money. Our educational system teaches us the fundamentals of math, English, and history; later on down the road we learn a trade or profession so that we can make money. But what's missing is what to DO with the money once we get it; how best to manage it and get the most out of every dollar so we can enjoy financial independence.

As a result, when they should be enjoying the fruits of their labor, many people spend their retirement years with fear in the pit of their stomachs. They become worried and anxious, and lose sleep at night. Living this way does nothing to help our relationships, our health, or our enjoyment of what should be one of the most fun and rewarding times in our lives. Whether the advice is free or cheap, if it doesn't add value to your life and get you to where you want to go, then it's expensive advice, indeed.

The year 2016 marks my 25th year in the financial industry as an independent investment advisor, and I am passionate about helping people protect their nest egg and what they have worked a lifetime to build. I believe that you can't have true success in life without addressing its many parts—physical, mental, financial, emotional, and spiritual. Each of these aspects are interconnected and impacts other aspects, much the way investment decisions impact tax and income decisions. It doesn't matter if you make it to retirement with plenty of money if you leave in your wake a trail of damaged or destroyed relationships. This can happen when decisions aren't made with the bigger picture in mind.

Retirement simply won't be much fun or fulfilling if you are unhealthy physically, emotionally, or spiritually. This is why I consider the principles of wise stewardship when designing sound financial plans. This book is here to help guide you on the road to financial independence so you can retire strong, with enough income and peace of mind to live happy and worry-free, no matter where your journey takes you.

## WHAT ARE THE FINANCIAL PRINCIPLES THAT YOU LIVE BY?

When The Good Lord created this earth He put into place certain **Physical Principles** that govern our physical world. For example, when you jump up in the air, you always come back down. It's called gravity, it's a principle, it's a law, and it happens every time you do it. Also, when you wake up in the morning, the sun is always rising in the east. Don't get up looking for it to rise in the west, because it is never going to happen.

Just as the Good Lord put into place physical principles that govern our physical world, He also put into place principles that govern our spiritual world. These governing laws or **Spiritual Principles** also come into play every time, and they tell us that *you will reap what you sow.* If you want love, you have to give love; if you want respect from others, you have to give respect to them; and if you want to live a positive life you to have to not only think, speak and act in positive ways, but you must surround yourself with other positive people. Like does attract like. So, just as The Good Lord put into place these Physical Principles that govern our physical world and these Spiritual Principals that govern our spiritual world, He put into place certain Financial Principals that govern our financial world. You can't violate these Financial Principles and expect things to turn out right any more than you can expect to defy gravity.

As good stewards, we have the responsibility to manage and protect the resources that we've been fortunate and diligent enough to accumulate. Hopefully, mere survival is not your idea of success. Many people are mistaken about how the financial principles that govern the investing world operate. You might have followed some of them to accumulate wealth when getting TO retirement, but as we mentioned earlier the strategies, tools and methodologies you need to get THROUGH retirement are different. To complicate matters even more, you can't use the same strategies that worked yesteryear for your grandparents or parents and expect to enjoy the same level of retirement they did. Retirement is quite unlike any financial challenge you've ever faced before. When solving this challenge, you have to remember that today, we live in a very different world.

## THIS IS NOT YOUR GRANDDADDY'S RETIREMENT

Retirement planning has gotten much harder than it used to be. While this news is a bit of a downer, it won't come as a surprise to most of you. We live in a much different financial world today than 20, 15 or even just 10 years ago. This book is here to give you a roadmap to follow so you can use the strength of proven financial principles along with the newer strategies and methodologies required to navigate the challenges brought about by the following three main changes:

- **Loss of the pension**: Most Boomers retiring today have their Social Security benefit and some amount of savings, but instead of a guaranteed pension, they have a 401(k) or similar plan. These plans offer you a way to participate in market gains, but they put all of the risk on you, the investor, without giving you the peace of mind that a pension can bring. Chapters 1, 2 and 3 tell you what you need to know about the investments inside of your 401(k) or IRA so you can effectively *create your own pension* using the new tools and strategies talked about in Chapter 6.

- **Entrance into a global economy**: The U.S. stock market is no longer just about America. What happens in China or Syria or Japan can affect the relative returns of the average U.S. investor, which means if you're a retiree relying on those investments for income, you will be in for a bumpy ride. As the volatility index in Chapter 2 shows us, we are no longer living during the heydays of the 1990s when interest rates were high and safe money investments paid out respectable rates. Chapter 7, *The Truth About Market Loss*, shows you what happens when you rely solely on market investments in today's climate of high market volatility and low interest rates on typical safe-money investments. To combat this, Chapter 8 shares the investment strategies of institutional money managers that give you a more secure way to capture growth opportunities during retirement.

- **Longer life expectancies**: Our grandparents who retired may have had it easy when it came to planning, but they also didn't have as many golden years to enjoy. The life expectancy at birth back in 1930 was a mere 58 years for men and 62 years for women, which meant most people felt lucky just getting to retirement!* According to the 2011 Social Security actuaries table, the average 65-year-old male today can expect to live another 17.6 years; the average 65-year old woman another 20 years.** Chapters 9 and 10 teach you the benefits of tax planning and tax allocation so you can effectively KEEP more of the dollars you worked so hard to earn.

---

\* *https://www.ssa.gov/history/lifeexpect.html*

\*\* *https://www.ssa.gov/oact/STATS/table4c6.html*

## GETTING TO VS. GETTING THROUGH RETIREMENT

Although the subject of this book is financial, achieving real success during retirement has more to do with your beliefs and your ability to adapt than it has to do with the accumulation of financial wealth. This might come as a surprise to many because we have been told over and over by the media and Wall Street that it's the SIZE of your account that matters and rate of returns rules all. Life is a school that presents us with circumstances and situations that allow us to grow, and this growth can help reshape incorrect beliefs, giving us the opportunity to adapt. You might think of the **Law of Life** as, *grow or die*, or, as the U.S. Marine Corps puts it: **improvise, adapt, and overcome.**

Retirement is one such time in your life that requires you to adapt, because **the financial principles that got you TO retirement are different from the ones that can get you successfully THROUGH retirement.** During your working years, you are getting TO retirement by working and saving. This is known in the financial industry as *the accumulation phase.* This is the phase you are leaving behind as you enter into retirement. Retirement is known as the *distribution phase.* How well you manage this distribution phase is what determines how well you will enjoy getting THROUGH retirement.

One of the biggest mistakes retirees are making today is entering the distribution phase with an investment strategy designed *only* to grow their money with no thought at all to the safe, effective and efficient distribution of these funds. There are many risks that retirees face as they enjoy their new longer periods of retirement. Some of the big ones include but are not limited to the following:

- **Spending too much during retirement:** Putting together a comprehensive income plan before retiring is critical. If you haven't created a budget and determined what your core expenses and provisional needs are, how can you create a financial plan with any certainty that it will meet your needs? You can't, which is why Chapter 4 of this book takes you through the process of creating a solid income plan.

- **Longevity risk:** We talked earlier about the increased life expectancy rates of men and women today. Not only can today's retirees expect to make it to age 65, but they'll still be going strong for many years after. About one out of every four 65 year-olds can expect to live past the age of 90, and one out of 10 will live past the age of 95.* These bonus years can be a blessing or a curse, depending on how well you plan.

- **Inflation:** Growing your savings so they can keep up with inflation isn't as easy as it once used to be. The low interest rates offered by safe investments such as bank CDs currently expose your money to a slow infestation that can be compared to termites. *Inflation eats away at your money even if it's in a "safe" investment.* This is yet another challenge faced by retirees today. The solution requires access to a full range of investments, strategies and methodologies that can act as effective fumigation against these and other termites.

- **Market risk:** Obviously no one can predict with accuracy when the market will fall or rise. I can promise you, however, that we will continue to see both bull and bear markets in the future. Chapter 1 of this book, *What Wall Street Won't Tell You About Retirement*, shows you how the numbers that once worked FOR you during your accumulation years now go to work AGAINST you during your distribution years unless you have a comprehensive income plan in place.

---

\* *http://ssa.gov/planners/lifeexpectancy.htm*

- **Risk of health care costs:** According to Healthview Services 2015 Retirement Health Care Costs Data Report, a couple aged 65 who retired in 2015 can expect to spend an estimated $266,000, during their retirement lifetime for basic health care services, and this cost is expected to rise to more than $320,000 in the next ten years.*
- **Unexpected event risk:** The risk list here includes the loss of spouse, long-term care costs, and caring for elderly parents. Are you more likely to receive care or to give care to a dependent family member? Did your grandfather live to be a hundred? Do you come from hardy stock and never get sick? Your beliefs about long-term care may not have anything to do with the realities of the situation faced by most retirees today. According to the U.S. Department of Health and Human Services, 70 percent of people turning age 65 can expect to use some form of long-term care during their lives.**

Because of these risks and many others, it's vital to the survival of your nest egg that you put together a comprehensive plan that provides both growth and a guaranteed source of income for your core needs. **It is the CASH flowing into your accounts that keeps the engine of your lifestyle running smoothly, which is why the focus of any good retirement plan should be on getting guaranteed paychecks for life.** It's not the million bucks that will give you peace of mind, because you can lose that million bucks just as easily as you can lose your way on a dark and rainy highway. From an investment standpoint, retirement is LESS about capital gain and MORE about cash flow. You see, during the accumulation phase the acronym "ROI" stands for "**return**

---

* *https://www.hvsfinancial.com/PublicFiles/Data_Release.pdf*
** *http://longtermcare.gov/the-basics/who-needs-care/*

**on investment"** but during the distribution phase its meaning changes to **"reliability of income."** It's cash flow that allows you to enjoy a strong retirement while living happy and worry-free, and that is what I am here to help you achieve.

## YOUR RETIREMENT GUIDE

What's the difference between a travel agent and a tour guide? Travel agents tell you where to go, whereas the tour guide takes you there. The travel agent stays behind their desk, the tour guide has been there many times before. Moreover, the travel agent makes recommendations based on what other people say, the tour guide makes recommendations based on fact and personal experience. Case in point: back in 2008 the media proclaimed that tech stocks were hot and brick and mortar establishments were dead. Anyone caught during that time chasing tech stocks and ignoring the fundamentals of sound financial principles got hurt when the tech bubble burst and the economy came crashing down. **Since then it has been my mission to make sure that no retiree ever runs the risk of losing their retirement hopes and dreams.** Having a solid plan in place means not only enjoying a guaranteed stream of income and a solid loss mitigation plan or "safety net" under your investments but also not having to go through the stress and pain and worry of *hoping* you have enough money.

ETS Financial Services works to provide individuals, families and businesses with innovative investment management solutions. We take pride in the fact that our clients have access to world class institutional money managers who focus on growing and protecting our clients' capital in both good and bad markets. We also offer access to CPAs and Estate Planning Attorneys to create customized retirement plans that allow you to reach your goals and achieve financial independence. When it comes to values, we always do the right thing, and that isn't just a promise, it's a legal responsibility we are held to as a fiduciary. We like to say that "ETS is where the Golden Rule *rules*".

This book is a culmination of the wisdom and advice from other financial mentors I've had the privilege of working with over the years, in addition to my own lessons learned and the experiences I have gained working with hundreds of clients over the years. The result is a guide I brought together so all my clients can enjoy the strongest, best retirement possible. For a current or aspiring retiree, I know that taking a loss doesn't just mean losing money; it means losing out on the opportunity to live the life you've always dreamed would be your golden years. What I want for you is what I want for all my clients—a strong, worry-free retirement.

Here's to being golden,

– *Eric Scoggins*, CFP®, Investment Advisor Representative and President ETS Financial Services.

# 1

# WHAT WALL STREET WON'T TELL YOU ABOUT RETIREMENT

*If what you thought was always true turned out to be wrong, when would you want to know about it?*

*Bill was born into an average middle-class family and had a good start in life. Although he was only an average student, Bill was bright and had a great work ethic. Not only did he finish high school, he also graduated from UGA after four years of college. He was by all accounts your average American male embarking on his journey to achieve the "The American Dream." He went to work right out of college and when he turned age 25, he landed a decent job that had potential. Not too long after that he got married, bought a home and started a family.*

*The year was 1991, and life was going pretty darn good. Bill worked hard at the office during the week, and on the weekends he spent quality time with his wife and kids. As a "Do It Yourselfer," Bill enjoyed the sense of pride that came with each home improvement project he completed. He was also a DIY investor and was interested in making all the right moves to plan for his financial future. Bill read financial publications, watched financial programs on T.V., and regularly listened to the most popular financial radio shows. Although he never took the time to call into any of the shows himself, he often took the free advice that was given to other callers because the advice seemed to make sense. He knew the radio host wasn't actually a licensed insurance or investment professional, but the advice sounded good and a lot of it reiterated what he read on the Internet and in magazines. Bill reasoned that the host was just confirming things he already knew to be true.*

*One thing that seemed to be true was that the tech industry was really growing. Bill reallocated 100 percent of his 401(k) account. He wanted to be smart, so he reallocated both his account balances and new contributions to several good funds in order to diversify because he knew enough not to put all of his eggs in one basket. Although Bill didn't really understand why his investments were doing well, he knew that everyone he spoke with (friends, family and his neighbor) heard and followed the same advice. He considered diversifying into other financial products, but just couldn't see the point, and besides, he couldn't take the embarrassment of his neighbor outperforming him.*

*Flash forward to the year 2000, when financial progress stalls. Although it didn't feel good losing 36 percent of the value of his portfolio in one year, it wasn't totally unexpected with all of the consecutive years of positive gains. But by the time October of 2001 came, Bill was becoming unnerved. He sustained another loss, yet his advisor encouraged him to stay in the market. Bill reminded him that he wanted to retire before he turned age 70; the advisor reminded him that as long as he stayed the course, what he had was just a "paper loss." Who could argue with that?*

*Still, at age 62, Bill felt like things were different now. Actually, he was becoming somewhat of a mental basket case and didn't know what to do.* **He was hearing a lot of financial noise on the T.V., noise from radio programs, friends, family and his advisor, yet he couldn't discern fact from fiction.** *Should he stay in the market or sell and get out? And if he did sell, what else should he get into? Bill couldn't sleep at night, was a distracted wreck, and even felt like he had developed ulcers. Who could he turn to for advice? Should he call into his favorite radio show and see if they could give him some advice? Would they to take the time to really understand his personal situation, his goals for retirement, his fears, concerns and his total financial picture?*

*And then one night around 2 a.m., it hits him: Wait a minute, those guys on the radio aren't even licensed to give financial advice, much less able to implement solutions!*

Money represents more than the paper it's printed on. It is the embodiment of your time, your talents, and your commitments. It buys the food you eat, the house you sleep in, the car you drive, and the clothes you wear. It also helps provide you with the lifestyle you want to live once you retire.

You have spent a lifetime earning it, spending it, and hopefully, accumulating it. When the time comes for retirement, you want your money to provide you with a comfortable lifestyle and stable income after your working days are done. You might also have other desires, such as traveling, purchasing property, or moving to be closer to your family (or farther away). You may also want your assets to provide for your loved ones after you are gone.

The truth is that it takes more than just money to fulfill those needs and desires. Your income, your plans for retirement, your future healthcare expenses, and the continued accumulation of your assets after you stop working and drawing a paycheck all rely on one thing: *You.* So what should you be doing with your money?

As the quote at the beginning of this chapter suggests, many people enter into retirement doing the wrong thing. As they come from their accumulation years, their portfolios are invested heavily in the stock market, in growth-mode investments. Many people like Bill are uncomfortable with maintaining this level of risk as they prepare for retirement, and so they start to wonder, "What else should I be doing?" The right answer will depend on your individual situation, the assets you currently own, your goals, risk tolerance and your retirement timeline. That's not the kind of advice you'll hear on the radio, read on the Internet, or hear in the news, however.

## WHY YOU DON'T WANT TO TAKE FINANCIAL ADVICE FROM THE MEDIA

Free advice is everywhere we turn. For people like Bill, or anyone who is nearing or preparing for retirement, the Internet and media does you a great disservice. It speaks of investment products and solutions in a way that leaves you needing more on multiple fronts. First, even experts who do have good intentions are often ignorant and lacking the professional education, licenses and experience necessary to implement the advice they give. Second, they are giving this advice without the relevant personal information necessary to determine whether or not the recommended product is in your best interest. That's a lot like recommending snow tires for everyone regardless of where they live and what kind of car they drive. But perhaps the biggest problem comes from the inherent conflict of interest when it comes to this kind of advice.

The magazines, websites and radio shows are all dispensing information in a biased way—in order to make a profit. **Their goal is to sell magazines, attract viewers, sell airtime, and sell**

**ads. Their goal is NOT to help you design a comprehensive financial plan.** They want you to read what they write, listen to what they say and buy what their sponsors recommend *because that's how they make money.*

Those who are planning today for a better financial future by using only free advice from unlicensed, non-professionals such as friends, family and radio personalities are no doubt missing out on the most effective planning opportunities available today. Advice about what to do with money has been around as long as money has existed. While there are basic financial principles that have stood the test of time, most strategies that work **adapt to changing conditions in the market**, in the economy and the world, as well as changes in your personal circumstances. The Great Recession of the early 2000's highlighted how old investment ideas were not only ineffective but incredibly destructive to the retirement plans of millions of Americans.

The reality is that investment strategies and savings plans that worked in the past have encountered challenging new circumstances that have turned them on their heads. Consider, for example, the 4-percent rule many people hear or read about in the media. The 4-percent rule basically tells you that it's fine to leave all your money in the market as long as you only take out 4-percent annually. However, due the volatility of our global economy and yields on government bonds and other "safe" money investments that are far below the historical averages, this rule no longer works. Morningstar Investment Management released a 2013 executive summary report with new findings that recommend a 2.8 percent withdrawal rate. That means if you have a $1 million portfolio, the most income you can safely take out is $28,000 a year. That's just a bit over $2,000 a month, and even living on that budget, your principal still isn't guaranteed.

The problem for many investors is discerning what the whole truth really is. We live in a difficult world where personal opinion cloaked as free advice is everywhere we turn. It is an age of information overload and oftentimes we are led to make financial decisions based on incorrect, biased or misleading information. How often have you heard phrases such as: "hold on, don't worry", "it's only a paper loss" and, "you don't want to sell now?" Unless you are using the word "loss" to describe the results of your current diet program, LOSS is *not* a good thing, especially during retirement. This chapter is here to show you exactly WHY.

## THE FLAW OF AVERAGES

Like a magician that uses sleight of hand to cover what's really going on, most brokers on Wall Street have you focused on the wrong thing. They show you *the average rate of return* and sell you on investments based on what they want you to see, but they don't show you the full picture. Imagine you have $100,000 to invest, and are given the choice between an investment portfolio that earns 11 percent and one that earns 6.7 percent. Which portfolio would you take?

Most people would sign up for the portfolio that earned 11 percent, and they would lose money. Why? Because they are looking at the wrong thing. What you have to ask is, *how did you arrive at that average 11 percent?* Using our example of $100,000, imagine the following three-year scenario:

- Year One: the investment LOSES 50 percent. Now you have $50,000.
- Year Two: the investment GAINS 50 percent. Now you have $75,000.
- Year Three: the investment GAINS 33 percent. Now you have $99,750.

**If you do the math, what you have is an average rate of return of 11 percent, yet you actually have LESS money than you started out with!**

Now let's look at our second option: a portfolio that averaged 6.7 percent rate of return. Using that same $100,000 investment, consider the following three-year scenario:

- Year One: the investment earns 0 percent. You still have $100,000.
- Year 2: the investment earns a 10 percent GAIN. You have $110,000.
- Year 3: the investment earns another 10 percent GAIN. You now have $121,000.

This gives us an average rate of return of 6.7 percent. Now which portfolio would you rather have? The one worth $99,750 or the one worth $121,000?

Losing big during the years just prior to or after retirement is so detrimental to your nest egg, we've devoted Chapter 7 to the reality of how loss affects a retirement. But first, let's take a closer look at the myth that says a loss on paper isn't a real loss until you sell the investment.

## WHY A PAPER LOSS IS A REAL LOSS

What you need to remember about loss in the stock market is simple: once you take a loss, you lose the ability to compound interest on that money forever. It was Albert Einstein who said, "Compound interest is the eighth wonder of the world. He who understands it, earns it. He who doesn't, pays it." Let's take a look at some trickier math to discover why this is true.

Imagine a 10-year time span where Investor A earns an average rate of 7.2 percent. One of the most basic financial principles is the Rule of 72 which tells us that at this rate of return, Investor A will double his money in 10 years. The math looks like this:

| YEAR: | TOTAL: |
|-------|--------|
| 0     | $1,000 |
| 1     | $1,072 |
| 2     | $1,149 |
| 3     | $1,232 |
| 4     | $1,321 |
| 5     | $1,416 |
| 6     | $1,518 |
| 7     | $1,627 |
| 8     | $1,744 |
| 9     | $1,870 |
| 10    | $2,004 |

Continue this for another 10 years, and Investor A will have $4,000 in 20-years' time. If you start out with $100,000 instead of just $1,000, you can see how nice it would be to double your money twice in a twenty-year period and end up with $400,000.

Now, let's take a look at what happens to the account balance when our investor loses just 8 percent during year three of his growth. That's not a very large loss, and it only happens once. While the investor doesn't sell and chooses to stay in the market, **this loss drastically changes how the investment compounds its returns.** Take a look at this math:

| YEAR: | TOTAL: |
|-------|--------|
| 0     | $1,000 |
| 1     | $1,072 |
| 2     | $1,149 |
| 3     | $1,057 (this is where the 8 percent loss occurs.) |
| 4     | $1,133 |
| 5     | $1,215 |
| 6     | $1,302 |

| YEAR: | TOTAL: |
|-------|--------|
| 7 | $1,396 |
| 8 | $1,497 |
| 9 | $1,604 |
| 10 | $1,720 |

Now our portfolio is worth $1,720 at the end of 10 years instead of $2,000, which means an 8 percent loss in year 3 equates to 14 percent less money in the end. **This loss isn't on paper, folks, it actually results in less money.** If we continue to grow this money for 20 years and never incur a loss again, we end up with $3,440, which is still 14 percent less than what we would have had if that loss in year three never occurred. **Even if you "hold on" and "ride it out" the loss is still REAL.** Add a few more zeros onto the end of the initial investment and you can see why this can be a real problem for retirees who need to rely on their investments for income during retirement. So the next time you are told "not to worry" about losses in your portfolio because they are only "paper losses" and that you are in it for "the long haul"; you can now dispel this Wall Street myth that has robbed millions of retirees of the ability to achieve their retirement dreams.

## A POP-QUIZ FOR YOUR FINANCIAL PROFESSIONAL

At this point, you might be wondering why your financial professional has never showed you math like this before. There is a pop-quiz you can give yourself to find out why. Don't worry, it's not a hard quiz; we'll use multiple choice. Ask yourself, **what do you think is the most important question to ask of any financial professional before deciding to trust him or her with the future of your retirement?**

- Question #1: How long have you been in the business?
- Question #2: What kind of fees do you charge?
- Question #3: Who do you work for?

- Question #4: What is your golf handicap?

While question number four is meant to be a little joke, most people still fail this quiz. How did you do? Did you guess the answer to be question number two? If you did, you would be wrong. While understanding the fees your financial professional charges is certainly important, you can really learn everything you need to know about fee structure, experience and work standards by finding out the answer to question number three: *Who do you work for?*

In the world of investing and finances, there are basically two different industry standards: the Suitability standard and the Fiduciary standard.

**Suitability standard.** If your advisor is not held to the fiduciary standard then they are not required to make recommendations that are in your best interest. Their recommendations just have to be "suitable" given your income, assets and risk tolerance. This allows your financial professional to recommend financial products that could be in their best interest rather than yours. If there are two products that do the same thing, and one of them pays out a higher commission fee to the professional, he or she is NOT legally obligated to disclose this information. Because these professionals work in-house for a name-brand company, they also have much less control over the kinds of products they can recommend to you. If their company doesn't have what you need, they can't get it for you, but they can sell you something that doesn't work as well and that generates higher revenue for them and their company.

**Fiduciary standard.** The fiduciary standard, on the other hand, requires that a financial professional always act in the best interest of his or her client at all times. Their loyalty isn't to the company they work for, but to YOU, their client. Investment

Advisor Representatives are held to the fiduciary standards of care and, as such, they have a legal obligation to:
- act in your best interest at all times
- be transparent about any conflict of interest
- help you to understand what you are buying and why
- properly align their interests with yours

Furthermore, professionals held to the fiduciary standard are typically independent professionals who don't work for a large firm or corporation. They work for their own independent firm. This offers an additional layer of security, because they can go anywhere to find the investment solutions that best fit your individual needs. Essentially, managing your money and your investments is an ongoing process that requires customization and adaptation to a changing world. And make no mistake; the world is always changing. What worked for your parents or even your parents' parents was probably good advice back then. People in retirement or approaching retirement today need new ideas and professional guidance.

## CHAPTER 1 QUICK TIPS //
- Evaluate whether or not you are following the RIGHT advice as you begin the retirement journey, and don't be afraid to do a financial U-turn before you get too far down the wrong road.
- Beware of the financial "noise" found on the internet, radio, TV and in financial magazines. All too often the so called "advice" you hear is merely someone's opinion and that "someone" may not even hold an insurance or securities license but freely dispenses "advice" to all who are within earshot.
- Choose to work with a Financial Professional who is held to the Fiduciary Standard.

# 2

# ORGANIZING YOUR ASSETS

*"Improvise, adapt, and overcome."*
*— U.S. Marine Corps*

Will your Social Security benefit, savings and other retirement assets be enough? If you're like Steve and Carol, you hope so. When the couple turned 60 years old, they started thinking about what their lives would be like in the next 10 years. When would they retire? What would their retirement look like? How much money did they have?

They could both count on Social Security benefits, but neither one really knew how much their monthly checks would be, or when to file for them. Steve had a modest pension that he could begin collecting at age 67. He had always hoped to retire before that age. Carol had a 401(k), but she honestly wasn't exactly sure how it worked, how she *could draw money from it and how much income it would provide once she retired.*

While Steve and Carol may sound like they're totally in the dark about their retirement, the truth is there are a lot of people just like them. They know retirement is coming and know they have some assets to rely on, but they aren't sure how it will all come together to provide them with a retirement income.

You spend your entire working life hoping what you put into your retirement accounts will help you live comfortably once you clock out of the workforce for good. The key word in that sentiment and the word that can make retirement feel like a looming problem instead of a rewarding life stage, is **hope**. You hope you'll have enough money. While I am a fan of both hope and prayer, when it comes to your retirement, the "hope & pray" plan is not recommended.

Leaving your retirement up to chance is unadvisable by nearly any standard, yet millions of people find themselves *hoping* instead of planning for a happy ending. Perhaps the most important lessons investors learned from the Great Recession is that not understanding where your money is invested (and the potential risks of those investments) can work against you, your plans for retirement and your legacy. Saving and investing money isn't enough to truly get the most out of it. You must have a planned approach to managing your assets.

## THE PURPOSE OF EVERY DOLLAR

From a purely financial perspective, the primary challenge of planning for a long, secure retirement is preparing for the day your paycheck stops and you need to turn a lifetime of savings into an income you cannot outlive. It is something quite unlike any financial challenge you have faced before. Most people who seek advice from a financial professional have done a good job of saving money. They have an investment plan, but not a retirement plan. *It's much more fun to plan for a trip rather than retirement, which is why people spend more time planning their vacations than they do planning for their retirement.* Without a plan, how do you know which bucket of money to draw from first? How do you hedge against inflation? How do you protect your spouse and subsidize their income when you pass away and they lose one Social Security check and the pension amount is cut in half? What if one of you has a long-term care event and either requires assistance at an assisted living facility or nursing home? Where will you get another $30,000 to $60,000 a year to fund long-term care costs?

*To build anything you need to have three things: a plan, a process, and the help of a professional.* Strong houses can't be built without blueprints; the same thing can be said of a strong retirement. Your lifestyle, your goals, and your idea of how you want to live are all factors that will shape the way you structure your investments to deliver the retirement you want.

This is another area where an investment advisor will approach things very differently than the typical broker working for the big bank, brokerage or box firms that are up and down the street. The way you invest during your peak earning years is different because your goals are different. Once you exit your accumulation phase, the money you saved becomes more important than ever before. In order to protect against the major risks we mentioned earlier, a financial professional held to fiduciary standards will want to sit down with you to get a better idea of who you are, your lifestyle, your goals and your plans for retirement.

**The purpose of the money will dictate the placement of the money.** For example, if long-term care is a high concern and a priority for you, then your investment advisor will fill you in on some of the lesser-known solutions available to retirees today. There are other tools available other than the traditional long-term care insurance. This type of insurance can be expensive and the premiums are not guaranteed so they can go up. Plus, you will have nothing to show for the premiums but cancelled checks if you wind up not needing the care. So, it is really a *use it or lose it* proposition. Many life insurance policies and annuity products have riders and provisions for increased income in the event of chronic illness. Often known as Living Benefits, these products provide you with an enhanced income amount to pay for home health care or a nursing home facility. The upside of these products is that should you never need the care, the money stays in your account and passes to your spouse or beneficiary. Even if it's too late to qualify for traditional long-term care insurance, long-term care riders on annuity and life insurance products might still be an option for you. Ask your investment advisor if this might be a solution appropriate for your situation and compare several options before making a decision. For example, Home Health Care or Nursing Home Confinement riders on annuities are not all built the same. Some have higher fees, others are built-in to the policy as an added benefit, and others may reduce the income payout once the annuity's accumulation value goes to zero. Nevertheless, these newer tools are very popular and might deserve another look because they offer more flexibility than traditional long-term care insurance.

## HOPE SO VS. KNOW SO MONEY

Now that you know there's more to saving and planning for retirement than filing for your Social Security benefit and drawing income from your 401(k), you can begin to **create a strategy for your retirement** that can have a significant impact on your financial landscape after you stop drawing a paycheck. Understanding how to manage your assets entails risk management, risk diversification, tax planning and income planning preparation throughout your life stages. These strategies can help you leverage more from each one of the hard-earned dollars you set aside for your retirement.

Let's take a look at some of the basic truths about money as it relates to saving for retirement.

There are essentially two kinds of money: *Hope So* and *Know So*. Everyone can divide their money into these two categories. Some have more of one kind than the other. The goal isn't to eliminate one kind of money but to balance them as you approach retirement.

**Hope So Money is money that is at risk.** It fluctuates with the market. It has no minimum guarantee. It is subject to investor activity, stock prices, market trends, buying trends, etc. You

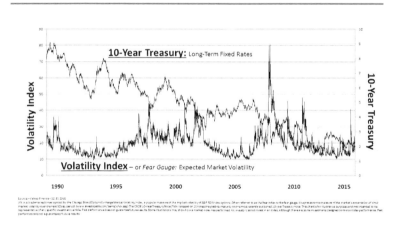

*The VIX, or volatility index, of the market represents expected market volatility. When the VIX Drops, economic experts expect less volatility. When the VIX rises, more volatility is expected.*

1. *VIX is a trademarked ticker symbol for the Chicago Board Options Exchange (CBOE) Market Volatility Index, a popular measure of the implied volatility of S&P 500 index options. Often referred to as the fear index or the fear gauge, it represents one measure of the market's expectation of stock market volatility over the next 30 day period. (wikipedia.com)*
2. *The CBOE 10-Year Treasury note (TNX) is based on 10 times the yield-to-maturity on the most recently auctioned 10-year Treasury note.*

get the picture. This money is exposed to more risk but also has the potential for more reward. Because the market is subject to change, you can't really be sure what the value of your investments will be worth in the future. You can't really *rely* on it at all. For this reason, we refer to it as Hope So Money. This doesn't mean you shouldn't have some money invested in the market, but it would be dangerous to assume you can know what it will be worth in the future.

Hope So Money is an important element of a retirement plan, especially in the early stages of planning when you can trade volatility for potential returns, and when a longer investment timeframe is available to you. In the long run, time can smooth out the ups and downs of money exposed to the market. Working with a professional and leveraging a long-term investment strategy has the potential to create rewarding returns from Hope So Money.

**Know So Money, on the other hand, is safer** when compared to Hope So Money. Know So Money is made up of dependable, low-risk or no-risk money, and investments that you can count on. Social Security is one of the most common forms of Know So Money. Income you draw or will draw from Social Security is guaranteed. You have paid into Social Security your entire career, and you can rely on that money during your retirement. Unlike the market, rates of growth for Know So Money are dependent on 10-year treasury rates. The 10-year treasury, or TNX, is commonly considered to represent a very secure and safe place for your money, hence Know So Money. The 10-year treasury drives key rates for things such as mortgage rates or CD rates. Know So Money may not be as exciting as Hope So Money, but it is safe.

Knowing the difference between Hope So and Know So Money is an important step towards a successful retirement plan. People who are 55 or older and who are looking ahead to retirement should be relying on more Know So Money than Hope So Money.

Ideally, the rates of return on Hope So and Know So Money would have an overlapping area that provided an acceptable rate of risk for both types of money. In the early 1990s, interest rates were high and market volatility was low. At that time, you could invest in either Hope So or Know So Money options because the rates of return were similar from both Know So and Hope So investments, and you were likely to be fairly successful with a wide range of investment options. At that time, you could expose yourself to an acceptable amount of risk or an acceptable fixed rate. Basically, it was difficult to make a mistake during that time period. Today, you don't have those options. Market volatility is at all-time highs while interest rates are at all-time lows. They are so far apart from each other that it is hard to know what to do with your money.

Yesterday's investment rules may not work today. Not only could they hamper achieving your goals, they may actually harm your financial situation. We are currently in a period when the rates for Know So Money options are at historic lows, and the volatility of Hope So Money is higher than ever. There is no overlapping acceptable rate, making both options less than ideal. *Because of this uncertain financial landscape, wise investment strategies are more important now than ever.*

This unique situation requires fresh ideas and investment tools that haven't been relied on in the past. Investing the way your parents did will not pay off. The majority of investment ideas used by financial professionals in the 1990s aren't applicable to today's markets. That kind of investing will likely get you in trouble and compromise your retirement. Today, you need a better PLAN.

## HOW MUCH RISK ARE YOU EXPOSED TO?

Many investors don't know how much risk they are exposed to. It is helpful to organize your assets so you can have a clear understanding of how much of your money is at risk and how much is in safer holdings. This process starts with listing all your assets.

Let's take a look at the two kinds of money:

**Hope So Money** is, as the name indicates, money that you *hope* will be there when you need it. Hope So Money represents what you would like to get out of your investments. Examples of Hope So Money include:

- Stock market funds, including index funds
- Mutual funds
- Variable annuities
- REITS

**Know So Money** is money that you know you can count on. It is safer money that isn't exposed to the level of volatility as the asset types noted above. You can more confidently count on having this money when you need it. Examples of Know So Money are:

- Government backed bonds
- Savings and checking accounts
- Fixed income annuities
- CDs
- Treasuries
- Money market accounts

> *» Scott had a modest brokerage account that he added to when he could. When he changed jobs a couple years ago, at age 58, Scott transferred his 401(k) assets into an IRA. Just a few years from retirement, he is now beginning to realize that nearly every dollar he has saved for retirement is subject to market risk.*

*Intuitively, he knows that the time has come to shift some assets to an alternative that is safer, but how much is the right amount?*

## INTRODUCING THE RULE OF 100

Determining the amount of risk that is right for you is dependent on a number of variables. You need to feel comfortable with where and how you are investing your money, and your financial professional is obligated to help you make decisions that put your money in places that fit your risk criteria.

Your retirement needs to first accommodate your day-to-day income needs. How much money do you need to maintain your lifestyle? When do you need it?

Managing your risk by having a balance of Hope So Money vs. Know So Money is a good start that will put you ahead of the curve. But how much Know So Money is enough to secure your income needs during retirement, and how much Hope So Money is enough to allow you to continue to benefit from an improving market?

In short, how do you begin to know how much risk you should be exposed to? While there is no single approach to investment risk determination advice that is universally applicable to everyone, there are some helpful financial principles that can be used as guidelines. One of the most useful is called *The Rule of 100*.

The average investor needs to accumulate assets to create a retirement plan that provides income during retirement and also allows for legacy planning. To accomplish this, they need to balance the amount of risk to which they are exposed. Risk is required because, while Know So Money is safer, more reliable and more dependable, it doesn't grow very fast, if at all. Today's historically low interest rates barely break even with current inflation. Hope So Money, while less dependable, has more potential for growth. Hope So Money can eventually become Know So Money once you move it to an investment with lower risk. Everyone's risk diversification will be different depending on their goals, age and their existing assets.

So how do you decide how much risk your assets should be exposed to? Where do you begin? Luckily, there's a guideline you can use to start making decisions about risk management. It's called the Rule of 100.

## HOW TO APPLY THE RULE TO FIND YOUR COMFORT ZONE

The Rule of 100 is a general rule that helps shape asset diversification* for the average investor. The rule states that the number 100 minus an investor's age equals the amount of assets they should have exposed to risk.

**The Rule of 100**: 100 − (your age) = the percentage of your assets that should be exposed to risk (Hope So Money)

For example, if you are a 30-year-old investor, the Rule of 100 would indicate that you should be focusing on investing primarily in the market and taking on a substantial amount of risk in your portfolio. The Rule of 100 suggests that 70 percent of your investments should be exposed to risk.

100 − (30 years of age) = 70 percent

Now, not every 30-year-old should have exactly 70 percent of their assets in mutual funds and stocks. The Rule of 100 is based on your chronological age, not your "financial age," which could vary

---

*Asset Diversification disclosure – Diversification and asset allocation does not assure of guarantee better performance and cannot eliminate the risk of investment loss. Before investing, you should carefully read the applicable volatility disclosure for each of the underlying funds, which can be found in the current prospectus.*

based on your investment experience, your aversion or acceptance of risk and other factors. While this rule isn't an ironclad solution to anyone's finances, it's a pretty good place to start. Once you've taken the time to look at your assets with a professional to determine your risk exposure, you can use the Rule of 100 to make changes that put you in a more stable investment position—one that reflects your comfort level.

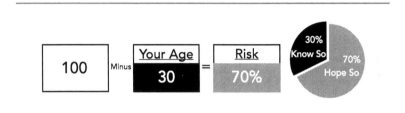

Perhaps when you were age 30 and starting your career, like in the example above, it made sense to have 70 percent of your money in the market: you had time on your side. You had plenty of time to save more money, work more and recover from a downturn in the market. Retirement was ages away, and your earning power was increasing. And indeed, younger investors should take on more risk for exactly those reasons. The potential reward of long-term involvement in the market outweighs the risk of investing when you are young.

Risk tolerance generally reduces as you get older, however. If you are 40 years old and lose 30 percent of your portfolio in a market downturn this year, you have 20 or 30 years to recover it. If you are 68 years old, you have much less time to make the same recovery. That new circumstance changes your whole retirement perspective. At age 68, it's likely that you simply aren't as interested in suffering through a tough stock market. There is less time to recover from downturns, and the stakes are higher. The money you have saved is money you will soon need to provide you with income, or is money that you already need to meet your income demands.

Much of the flexibility that comes with investing earlier in life is related to *compounding*. Compounded earnings can be incredibly powerful over time. The longer your money has time to compound, the greater your wealth will be. This is what most people talk about when they refer to putting their money to work. This is also why the Rule of 100 favors risk for the young. If you start investing when you are young, you can invest smaller amounts of money in a more aggressive fashion because you have the potential to make a profit in a rising market and you can harness the power of compounding earnings.

You risk not having a recovery period the older you get, so should have less of your assets at risk in volatile investments. You should shift with the Rule of 100 to protect your assets and ensure that they will provide you with the income you need in retirement. Let's look at another example that illustrates how the Rule of 100 becomes more critical as you age. An 80-year-old investor who is retired and is relying on retirement assets for income, for example, needs to depend on a solid amount of Know So Money. The Rule of 100 says an 80-year-old investor should have a maximum of 20 percent of his or her assets at risk. Depending on the investor's financial position, even less risk exposure may be required. You are the only person who can make this kind of determination, but the Rule of 100 can help. Everyone has their own level of comfort. Your Rule of 100 results will be based on your values and attitudes as well as your comfort with risk.

The Rule of 100 can apply to overarching financial management and to specific investment products that you own as well. Take the 401(k) for example. Many people have them, but not many people understand how their money is allocated within their 401(k). An employer may have someone who comes in once

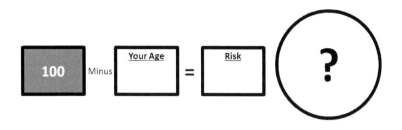

a year and explains the models and options that employees can choose from, but that's as much guidance as most 401(k) holders get. Many 401(k) options include target date funds that change their risk exposure over time, essentially following a form of the Rule of 100. Selecting one of these options can often be a good move for employees because they shift your risk as you age, securing more Know So Money when you need it.

A financial professional can look at your assets with you and discuss alternatives to optimize your balance between Know So and Hope So Money.

## CHAPTER 2 QUICK TIPS //

- The Rule of 100 is an age-old financial principle that has been around for a long time. You may be more conservative or more aggressive than what the Rule of 100 suggests, which is why it's important to work with a financial professional in order to determine an allocation that's appropriate for you.
- If you are retired or five to ten years away from retirement, it is critical that you have the appropriate asset allocation, because you simply do not have the time to make up for large market losses.
- Embrace change. As you begin to transition from the accumulation phase to the distribution phase of your life, things change. For example, the acronym "ROI" during the accumulation phase it stands for "Return on Investment". However, as you transition into the distribution phase, it changes and "ROI" now stands for "Reliability of Income".

# 3
# WHAT IS THE COLOR
# OF YOUR MONEY?

*"Divide your investment among many places for you
do not know what risks might lie ahead."*
*– King Solomon, Ecclesiastes 11:2*

Over the course of your lifetime, it is likely that you have acquired a variety of assets. Assets can range from money that you have in a savings account or a 401(k), to a pension or an IRA. You have earned money and have made financial decisions based on the best information you had at the time. When viewed as a whole, however, you might not have an overall strategy for the management of your assets. As we have seen, it's more important than ever to know which of your assets are at risk. High market volatility and low treasury rates make for challenging financial topography. Navigating this financial landscape starts with thoughtful asset management that takes into account your specific needs and options.

Even if you feel that you have plenty of money in your 401(k) or IRA, not knowing how much *risk* those investments are exposed to can cause you major financial suffering. Take the market crash of 2008 for example. In 2008, the average diversified stock fund fell by 38 percent.* Those retirees and pre-retirees who took the "advice" of one popular radio host fared even worse. Although I am not aware of this host being professionally licensed to actually give investment advice, he seems to recommend that his listeners invest into the Vanguard Index 500. His reasoning was that it held a, "diversified portfolio of blue chip stocks" and because it also had "very low fees". Sadly, those listeners who took that generic "advice" wound up being "penny wise and pound foolish". Although they may have saved some money in fees, they sat completely paralyzed due to extreme fear as they helplessly watched their dreams of retirement quickly evaporate when the fund lost 52.4 percent of its value from October 2007 to February 2009 in a blink of an eye!

Because of this type of "advice" and the constant conditioning of Wall Street, her army of advisors, the financial press and the media at large (their propaganda partners), it is usually the main street investors, especially retirees and pre-retirees, who end up suffering the most.

We are constantly told that "losses in our portfolios are not actually losses but simply paper losses" and "that we won't realize any loss until we actually sell" and "if we sell, not only are we wimps, but we can never recover, and besides, we are in it for…(go ahead and finish for me)…that's right—"the long haul". Sounds logical doesn't it? But this type of "advice" is not only bad and

---

* http://www.wsj.com/articles/SB10001424127887324682204578513340507532544

untrue as we discussed in Chapter 1, it can also be detrimental to your retirement dreams and, more importantly, your health. Countless individuals lived in tremendous fear during the crisis of 2008, when they were torn between listening to their gut that was screaming, "Take action! Protect your nest egg!" versus the advice from Wall Street screaming, "Buy and hold! You're in it for the long haul!" This caused stress, depression, ulcers, and many sleepless nights for those who lost hope and paid the ultimate price—the loss of what took a lifetime to build.

It's been said that "Bad Breath is better than no breath," but NO ADVICE is certainly better than bad advice!

If more people had shifted their investments away from risk as they neared retirement age (i.e. the Rule of 100), they may have lost a lot less money going into retirement. One of the easiest ways to understand the risk inside your current investment portfolio is to use a color system for your money.

## THE COLOR OF MONEY

We use the colors red, green and yellow to identify the different levels of risk your investments are exposed to. Each color has unique benefits and features.

- Green Money is known as safe money, because it is money that has a contractual guarantee of principal. While no investment is completely without risk, these investments employ safer strategies for income protection during retirement. Green Money is money that you know you can count on. It is safer money that isn't exposed to the level of volatility as the asset types noted below. You can more confidently count on having this money when you need it.
- Red Money is known as risk money. These investments are exposed to the risk and fluctuation of the stock market, but they provide growth opportunities for your

money. Red Money represents money that has potential to both grow and lose value. It is exposed to 100 percent of both the upside and downside of the markets without any safety net under it, thus you could lose it all.

- Yellow Money is institutionally managed money. It is still at risk, but it is controlled risk, money that is managed from a loss mitigation perspective. We will go into more depth about managed money in Chapter 8.

| Green Money | Red Money | Yellow Money |
|---|---|---|
| "Green Money" is safer. | "Red Money" is at risk. | "Yellow Money" is controlled risk. |
| This is money that offers a minimum guarantee but it may pose risks other than market risk. | This is money that can go up or down in value. It may pose risk if it is not properly managed to serve a specific purpose in a comprehensive plan. | Yellow Money is institutionally managed money under the watchful eye of a professional. |

The fact of the matter is that a lot of people don't know their level of exposure to risk. Visually organizing your assets is an important and powerful way to get a clear picture of what kind of money you have, where it is and how you can best use it in the future. This process is as simple as listing your assets and assigning them a color. Work with your financial professional to create a comprehensive inventory of your assets to understand what you are working with before making any decisions. This may be the first time you have ever sat down and sorted out all of your assets, allowing you to see how much money you have at risk in the market. A lot of people are surprised to find how much of their portfolio is actually in Red Money investments. A lot of this has to do with the many misconceptions out there about market investments and myths often perpetuated as sound financial advice.

## FOUR MAJOR MYTHS AND MISCONCEPTIONS ABOUT WEALTH MANAGEMENT

In the financial industry there are countless myths, misconceptions and half-truths that we are spoon-fed nearly every day. One of the goals of this book is to help you wade through all of the financial noise. We are now going to pull back the curtain, so to speak, and give you the insider's picture so you can understand why these myths have been perpetuated over time and who they actually benefit. Once you learn more about the man behind the curtain, who he or she is, where their loyalty lies, and the math they use to convince you to do what often seems counterintuitive, you'll be better able to stay on the road to financial independence.

- **MYTH #1: The best way to grow wealth and create income during retirement is to invest in a diversified portfolio of mutual funds**: People typically buy into equities for growth and bonds for safety, but as the Color of Money shows us, both are actually Red Money. There are many different kinds of bonds—short-term government bonds, high-yield junk bonds—and different degrees of risk within these bonds. These risks include credit risk, default risk and interest rate risk. Many people buy into the idea that a traditional 60/40 mixed portfolio of bonds to stocks is safe, but the truth is you CAN lose money in bonds. If interest rates go up, the bond value goes down. In addition, dividend and interest payments are not guaranteed and can fluctuate. So your income stream is at the mercy of the fluctuations of the markets, which means when the markets change you may have to adjust your lifestyle. Today's retirees have much better options such as Green Money indexed products for the guaranteed portion of their portfolio and Yellow Money options provided by institutional money managers that give greater risk mitigation.

- **MYTH #2: When the market crashes, just hang in there, suck it up, and stay for the long haul:** We've already talked about how we hear all the time that when the market falls, you haven't really lost anything because it's just a paper loss. In Chapter 1, we did the math that demonstrated why this saying simply isn't true. Once that money goes out of your account, you can't compound on that money again. This is especially detrimental to retirees who can't earn that money back, which is why you want to take care to avoid too much exposure to risk more than ever during retirement.

- **MYTH #3: Never buy an annuity or cash value life insurance.** You might say that BAD breath is better than NO breath, but you might also say that NO advice is better than BAD advice, especially when it comes to the security of your retirement. Be wary of anyone—financial professional or otherwise—who demonizes certain financial products. Investments by themselves are neither good nor bad until they are put to use. It's applying them to the wrong situation that can make them dangerous to the future of your retirement. Think of them as tools in the tool box. You would never say that a hammer is a piece of garbage or a rip-off unless you were recommended to buy it and foolish enough to try it for digging a hole. Conversely, you wouldn't want to use a shovel to pound a nail in the wall. Each tool in the box serves its purpose just as certain financial tools are better suited to solve certain problems than others. When someone demonizes a financial tool, it usually means they either don't understand how to apply that tool, or they don't have the ability to get you that tool. A professional held to fiduciary standards has a deeper toolbox than most professionals because they are not working for a captive company. Their job is to discover what financial tools can best help you meet your goals. Do you need a saw, a screwdriver, or a hammer to build a house? The answer is you need all three.

- **MYTH #4: The only way to get a reasonable rate of return on your money is to risk that money in the stock market.** As a retiree facing the risk of running out of money, market volatility, inflation, rising healthcare and low interest rates, your gut is telling you that you have to protect your money. Wall Street, your broker and their propaganda partners, however, are telling you something different. They want you to stay fully invested because they cannot collect fees on money you don't keep invested. So the brokers will show you slick charts that illustrate how if you "panic" and jump out (of the market not the window) and then subsequently miss the best 10, 20, or 30 days in a particular market cycle, then what would have been some really nice performance rates would instead become negative returns. So the moral of that story is probably familiar: you must "buy & hold," take your lumps, and stay in it for the long haul because you can't time the market. If you look at what happens when you miss out on the best days, the math of those numbers might convince you that they are right.

  But wait just a minute—before you bet the farm, you need to know that there is another way to look at the numbers. As a retiree entering distribution mode, you need to be more concerned about what happens when you are in the market during the worst days. Take a look at Chapter 7: *The Truth About Loss During Retirement*, to see what the numbers have to say about loss and then decide for yourself. You don't have to keep your nest egg in Red Money investments in order to earn good returns during retirement.

The way you organize your assets depends on your goals and your level of comfort with risk. Whatever you determine the appropriate amount of risk for you to be, you will need to organize your portfolio to reflect your goals. If you have more Red Money than Green Money, in particular, you will need to make decisions about how to move it. You can work with a financial professional to find appropriate Green Money options for your situation.

The next step is to know the right amount and ratio of Green and Red Money for you at your stage of retirement planning. **Investing heavily in Red Money and gambling ALL of your assets on the market is incredibly risky no matter where you fall within the Rule of 100.** Money in the market can't be depended on to generate income, and a plan that leans too heavily on Red Money can easily fail, especially when investment decisions are influenced by emotional reactions to market downturns and recoveries. Not only is this an unwise plan, it can be incredibly stressful to an investor who is gambling everything on stocks and mutual funds.

**But a plan that uses too much traditional Green Money tools avoids all volatility and can also fail.** Why? Investing all of your money in Certificates of Deposit (CDs), savings accounts, money markets and other low return accounts may provide interest and income, but that likely won't be enough to keep pace with inflation. If you focus exclusively on income from traditional Green Money tools and avoid owning any stocks or mutual funds in your portfolio, you won't be able to leverage the potential for long-term growth your portfolio needs to stay healthy and productive. Also, today there are newer, more productive Green Money tools available. These newer tools have higher upside potential than the traditional Green Money tools that have been available for retirement planning in the past. This is where the Rule of 100 can help you determine how much of your money should be invested in the market to anticipate your future needs.

Green Money becomes much more important as you age. While you want to reduce the amount of Red Money you have and to transition it to Green Money, you don't necessarily need all of it to generate income for you right away. Taking a closer look at your money, you will see that you need different amounts at different times.

## TYPES OF MONEY:
### NEED NOW AND NEED LATER

Money that you need to depend on for income is Green Money. Once you have filled the income gap at the beginning of your retirement, you may have money left over.

*There are two types of Money:* money used for income now and money used for accumulation to meet your income needs in five, 10 or 20 years.

**Money needed for income is Need Now Money.** It is money you need to meet your basic needs, to pay your bills, your mortgage if you have one and the costs associated with maintaining your lifestyle. It was Tom Hegna who coined the term "paychecks and playchecks." Your Need Now Money is your paycheck money.

**Money used for accumulation is Need Later Money.** This is money that you don't need now for income, but will need to rely on down the road. You might think of this as your playcheck money. When the market is doing good, you say great! And you go out and have some extra fun. When the market is doing poorly, you still have those reliable paychecks coming in, so you don't have to worry. Need Later Money might also represent income your assets will need to generate for future use. When planning your retirement, it is vital to decide how much of your assets to structure for income now and how much to set aside to accumulate to create Need Later Money.

You must figure out if your core income and accumulation needs are met. Your Need Now and Need Later Money are top priorities. Need Now Money, in particular, will dictate what your options for future needs are.

## OPTIMIZING RISK AND FINDING THE RIGHT BALANCE

Determining the amount of risk that is right for you depends on your specific situation. It starts by examining your particular financial position.

The Rule of 100 is a useful way to begin to deliberate the right amount of risk for you. But remember, it's just a baseline. Use it as a starting point for figuring out where your money should be. If you're a 50-year-old investor, the Rule of 100 suggests that you have 50 percent Green Money and 50 percent Red Money. Most 50-year-olds are more risk tolerant, however. There are many reasons why someone might be more risk tolerant, not the least of which is feeling young! Experienced investors, people who feel they need to gamble for a higher return, or people who have met their retirement income goals and are looking for additional ways to accumulate wealth are all candidates for investment strategies that incorporate higher levels of risk. In the end, it comes down to your personal tolerance for risk. How much are you willing to lose?

Consulting with a financial professional is often the wisest approach to calculating your risk level. A professional can help determine your risk tolerance by getting to know you, asking you a set of questions and even giving you a survey to determine your comfort level with different types of risk. Here's a typical scenario a financial professional might pose to you:

*"You have $100,000 saved that you would like to invest in the market. There is an investment product that could turn your $100,000 into $120,000. That same option, however, has the potential of losing you up to $30,000, leaving you with $70,000."*

Is that a scenario that you are willing to enter into? Or are you more comfortable with this one:

*"You could turn your $100,000 into $110,000, but have the potential of losing $15,000, leaving you with $85,000."*

Your answer to these and others types of questions will help a financial professional determine what level of risk is right for you. They can then offer you investment strategies and management plans that reflect your financial age.

## THE NUMBERS DON'T LIE

When the rubber meets the road, the numbers dictate your options. Your risk tolerance is an important indicator of what kinds of investments you should consider, but if the returns from those investments don't meet your retirement goals, your income needs will likely not be met. For example, if the level of risk you are comfortable with manages your investments at a 4 percent return and you need to realize an 8 percent return, your income needs aren't going to be met when you need to rely on your investments for retirement income. A professional may encourage you to be more aggressive with your investment strategy by taking on more risk in order to give you the potential of earning a greater return. If taking more risk isn't an option that you are comfortable with, then the discussion will turn to how you can earn more money or spend less in order to align your needs with your resources more closely.

How are you going to structure your income flow during retirement? The answer to this question dictates how you determine your risk tolerance. If the numbers say that you need to be more aggressive with your investing, or that you need to modify your lifestyle, it becomes a choice you need to make.

## CHAPTER 3 QUICK TIPS //

- Look for a fiduciary professional who has access to not just accumulation tools, but all the tools in the tool box, both offense and defense.
- Beware of brokers who use an antiquated version of the Rule of 100 that still exposes 100 percent of your money to varying levels of risk. The old model only uses Stocks, Bonds and Alternatives Investments. All of these instruments are still Red Money and at risk and as such they do not have a contractual guarantee of principal.

# 4

# CREATING A SOLID INCOME PLAN

*"If your Outgo exceeds your Income, then Upkeep will be your Downfall."*
*— Attributed to the 20th century philosopher William Earl*

Take a moment to think about your income goals:
- What is your lifestyle today?
- Would you like to maintain it into retirement?
- Are you meeting your needs?
- Are you happy with your lifestyle?
- What do you really *need* to live on when you retire?

Some people will have the luxury of maintaining or improving their lifestyle, while others may have to make decisions about what they need versus what they want during their retirement.

But everyone regardless of their income needs can benefit from having a written plan.

## HOW MANY PEOPLE HAVE A WRITTEN INCOME PLAN?

How many of you reading this book are working with a broker or financial advisor? How many of you have a written income plan designed to help you manage the risk of running out of money? **Your provisional income** is the amount you need to land in your bank account every month come hell or high water to take care of your monthly provisions. This is your "Need Now" paycheck money, which is why this money needs to come from guaranteed sources that are as reliable as possible.

Organizing your assets, understanding the color of your money, and creating an income and accumulation plan for retirement can quickly become an overwhelming task. Finding the most efficient and beneficial way to address your core income needs will have an impact on your lifestyle, your asset accumulation and your legacy planning after you retire. Once you have identified your income need, you will know how much to carve off and protect for income generation and how much to set aside for accumulation.

The fact of the matter is that financial professionals build their careers around understanding the different variables affecting financing. You might have a million dollars socked away in a savings account, but your neighbor, who has $300,000 in a diverse investment portfolio with both "Red" and "Green" Money investments that are tailored to their exact provisional income needs, may end up enjoying a better retirement lifestyle. Why? They had more than a good work ethic and a penchant for saving. They have the peace of mind and security that can only come from guaranteed income streams, just like the retirees of the past who had the good fortune of having a personal pension. It's not the size of account value that brings peace of mind to retirees, but the amount of guaranteed lifetime income they have.

## HOW MUCH AND WHEN?

Every financial strategy for retirement needs first to accommodate the day-to-day need for income. The moment your working income ceases and you start living off the money you've set aside for retirement is referred to as the **retirement cliff**. When you begin drawing income from your retirement assets, you have entered the distribution phase of your financial life. *The distribution phase of your retirement plan* is when you reach the point of relying on your assets for income. This is where your Green Money comes into play: the safer, more reliable assets that you have accumulated that are designed to provide you with a steady income. On day one of your retirement, you will need a steady and reliable supply of income from your Green Money.

Satisfying that need for daily income entails first knowing *how much you need* and *when you will need it.*

**How Much Money Do You Need?** While this amount will be different for everyone, the general rule of thumb is that a retiree will require 70 to 80 percent of their pre-retirement income to maintain their lifestyle. We have many clients who are planning to replace 100 percent of their pre-retirement income, at least for the first five to ten years of their retirement, which I call the "Go-Go Years". As they enter their late 70s and early 80s, or the "Slow Go" years, they most likely will not be as active and will pare down their discretionary spending until they hit their late 80s and 90s, or the "No Go" years. Once you know what that number is, the key becomes matching your income need with the correct investment strategies, options and tools to satisfy that need.

**When Do You Need Your Money?** If you need income to last 10 years, use a tool that creates just that. If you need a lifetime of income, seek a tool that will do that and won't run out. When you take health care costs, potential emergencies, plans for moving or traveling, and other retirement expenses into account, you can really give your calculator a workout. You want to maximize retirement benefits to meet your lifetime income needs. An Investment Advisor can help you answer those questions by working with you to customize an income plan.

As we determined earlier in Chapter 1, the most important thing you need to do as you create an income plan is to take care to avoid too much exposure to risk. You can start by meeting with an Investment Advisor to organize your assets. Get your Green Money and Red Money in order and balanced to meet your needs. If the market goes down 18 percent this afternoon, you don't want that to come out of what you're relying on for next year's income. Hot on the heels of securing your Green Money, it's time to structure those Green Money assets so they can generate income for you. Ultimately, you have to take care of your monthly income needs to pay the bills.

The Big Kahuna of Green Money is your Social Security benefit. One vital aspect of a solid income plan for married couples is to consider what would happen to your income were one of you to pass away. Social Security is a lifelong benefit, but it ends when a person dies. For married couples, it is especially vital to the strength of your income plan to figure out how to replace any missing income that results from unexpected life events.

> *» Lee and Ann were high school sweethearts. They did everything together—went to the prom, got married, started a career, and had a family. After the kids were off to college and starting their own lives, Lee and Ann paid off the house and retired together at the age of 66.*
>
> *They felt pretty good about their financial future. Lee received a pension from his job that kicked in at the age of 67 in the amount of $36,000 a year. He also had $24,000 a year*

*coming to him from Social Security benefits. Ann's job did not give her a pension, but she had some money in a 401(k) plan invested in the stock market, and she was receiving $15,000 a year from Social Security benefits. They wanted to know how to best utilize Ann's investment money, so they went in to talk to a financial professional who specialized in income planning. What he showed them really opened their eyes!*

*First, the professional revealed what would happen were Lee to pass away at the age of 70. Not only would his wife lose her husband, she would also lose his pension check and one Social Security benefit check. Her income would drop from $75,000 a year to $42,000 a year! If she got sick or needed long-term care, she wouldn't be able to afford the $63,000 a year listed as the average cost of a nursing home in the state of Georgia.\* If she was healthy and lived a good life until the age of 85, Ann would still lose out on $495,000 of income. None of this sounded too appealing to Ann. She knew that chances were good Lee would go before her—everyone knew women tended to live longer than men—but she would still have the same bills to pay, plus she would have to hire somebody to mow the lawn!*

*Next, the professional showed them the good news. Using his "Income for Life" software, he ran the numbers and suggested how much and where to invest Ann's 401(k) money to carve out another $30,000 a year of guaranteed income for both of their lives. The investment was protected from market risk, and both she and Lee could use this money whenever they needed to "turn on" an additional income stream or tap into the account value. Meanwhile, the money would grow in a protected vehicle, earning more than enough to keep up with inflation. If they never needed to turn on that income*

---

\* *http://longtermcare.gov/cost-of-care-results/?state=US-GA*

*stream, then all the money would pass on to their children. Ann and Lee left that meeting with a written income plan and smiles on their faces. They no longer had to worry about market risk, inflation and the risk of unexpected events.*

Some retirees like Lee and Ann count on a pension income received by a spouse. With traditional defined-benefit pension plans, that income goes away when the person passes away unless you make provisions. Social Security is another type of defined-benefit plan that ends once a person passes away, but spousal benefits give you the option to choose the larger of the two benefit amounts. When this happens, you will only be getting one check, when before you were getting two. If you lose a pension income on top of it, then your paycheck could take a pretty severe cut. What's more, this pay cut remains in effect for the rest of your life. How would this affect your ability to meet your core expenses?

There are newer types of annuities on the market today like the one used by Lee and Ann in our story above to create their very own personal pension. These unique tools can provide an income stream for both you and your spouse, access to the cash value, and money to your beneficiaries in the event that you pass away. Ask your financial professional if he or she can help you complete a written income plan that will deliver you (and your spouse if you are married) strong paychecks for the rest of your life.

From an income standpoint, one of the easiest ways to address spousal continuation begins with a benefit that you have already paid into: Social Security. You have been paying into this benefit your entire life and it can provide the foundation for your income needs. Read on to learn how to get the most out of this Green Money income benefit.

## CHAPTER 4 QUICK TIPS //

- Armies have battle plans, builders have blueprints, and financial professionals have written income plans. Don't skip this step. Get a plan, anticipate the obstacles, and avoid the pull of the crowd. My mom always said: "Following the crowd leads nowhere"!
- Annuities are like doctors—there are both good and bad ones out there. By doing your due diligence and finding out where the good ones are, you'll have a much better chance of maintaining both good physical and financial health!

# 5

# GETTING THE MOST OUT OF SOCIAL SECURITY

It's not an entitlement, it is your money! You paid into the system all of your working life. Make sure the politicians never forget that fact!

One kind of Green Money that most Americans rely on for income when they retire is Social Security. If you're like most Americans, Social Security is or will be an important part of your retirement income and one that you should know how to properly manage. As a first step in creating your income plan, a financial professional will take a look at your Social Security benefit options. Social Security is the foundation of income planning for anyone who is about to retire and is a reliable source of Green Money in your overall income plan.

*» Sandra had worked full-time nearly her entire adult life and was looking forward to enjoying retirement with her husband, kids and grandkids. When she turned 62, she decided to take advantage of her Social Security benefits as soon as they became available.*

*A couple of years later, she was organizing some of the paperwork in her home office. She came across an old Social Security statement, and remembered the feeling of filing and beginning a new phase in her life.*

*However, as she looked over the statement, she realized in retrospect that she might have been better off waiting to file for benefits. She had saved enough to wait for benefits, and if she had, her monthly benefit could have been quite a bit more.*

*When she was in the process of retiring, there were so many other decisions to make. It seemed very straightforward to file right away. She made a note to call the Social Security Administration to see if it was possible to change her monthly benefit to the larger amount.*

Here are some facts that illustrate how Americans currently use Social Security:

- Nearly 90 percent of Americans age 65 and older receive Social Security benefits.*
- Social Security provides about 39 percent of the income of the elderly.*
- Claiming Social Security benefits at the wrong time can reduce your monthly benefit by up to 65 percent.**

---

\* *http://www.ssa.gov/pressoffice/basicfact.htm*

\** *https://www.ssa.gov/planners/retire/retirechart.html*

- In 2013, 36 percent of men and 40 percent of women claimed Social Security benefits at age 62.*
- In 2013, more than a third of workers claimed Social Security benefits as soon they became eligible.*
- In 2015, the average monthly Social Security benefit was $1,328. *The maximum benefit for 2015 was $2,663. The $1,335 monthly benefit reduction between the average and the maximum is applied for life.* \*\*

There are many aspects of Social Security that are well known and others that aren't. When it comes time for you to cash in on your Social Security benefit, you will have many options and choices. Social Security is a massive government program that manages retirement benefits for millions of people. Experts spend their entire careers understanding and analyzing it. Luckily, you don't have to understand all of the intricacies of Social Security to maximize its advantages. You simply need to know the best way to manage your Social Security benefit. You need to know exactly what to do to get the most from your Social Security benefit and when to do it. Taking the time to create a roadmap for your Social Security strategy will help ensure that you are able to exact your maximum benefit and efficiently coordinate it with the rest of your retirement plan.

There are many aspects of Social Security that you have no control over. You don't control how much you put into it, and you don't control what it's invested in or how the government manages it. However, you do control when and how you file for benefits. The real question about Social Security that you need to

---

\* *Trends in Social Security Claiming, Alicia H Munnell and Anqi Chen, Center for Retirement Research, May 2015. http://crr.bc.edu/wp-content/uploads/2015/05/IB_15-8.pdf*

\*\* *https://www.ssa.gov/news/press/factsheets/colafacts2015.html*

answer is, "When should I start taking Social Security?" While this is the all-important question, there are a couple of key pieces of information you need to track down first.

Before we get into a few calculations and strategies that can make all the difference, let's start by covering the basic information about Social Security which should give you an idea of where you stand. Just as the foundation of a house creates the stable platform for the rest of the framework to rest upon, your Social Security benefit is an important part of your overall retirement plan. The purpose of the information that follows is not to give an exhaustive explanation of how Social Security works, but to give you some tools and questions to start understanding how Social Security affects your retirement and how you can prepare for it.

Let's start with eligibility.

**Eligibility.** Understanding how and when you are eligible for Social Security benefits will help clarify what to expect when the time comes to claim them.

To receive retirement benefits from Social Security, you must earn eligibility. In almost all cases, Americans born after 1929 must earn 40 quarters of credit to be eligible to draw their Social Security retirement benefit. In 2015, a Social Security credit represents $1,220 earned in a calendar quarter. The number changes as it is indexed each year, but not drastically. In 2014, a credit represented $1,200. Four quarters of credit is the maximum number that can be earned each year. In 2015, an American would have had to earn at least $4,880 to accumulate four credits. In order to qualify for retirement benefits, you must have earned a minimum number of credits. Additionally, if you are at least 62 years old and have been married to a recipient of Social Security benefits for at least 12 months, you can choose to receive Spousal Benefits. Although 40 is the minimum number of credits required to begin drawing benefits, it is important to know that once you claim your Social Security benefit, there is no going back. Although there may be cost of living adjustments made, you are locked into that base benefit amount forever.

**Primary Insurance Amount.** You can think of your Primary Insurance Amount (PIA) like a ripening fruit. It represents the amount of your Social Security benefit at your Full Retirement Age (FRA). Your benefit becomes fully ripe at your FRA, and will neither reduce nor increase due to early or delayed retirement options. If you opt to take benefits before your FRA, however, your monthly benefit will be less than your PIA. You will essentially be picking an unripened fruit. On the one hand, waiting until after your FRA to access your benefits will increase your benefit beyond your PIA. On the other hand, you don't want the fruit to over ripen, because every month you wait is one less check you get from the government.

**Full Retirement Age.** Your FRA is an important figure for anyone who is planning to rely on Social Security benefits in their retirement. Depending on when you were born, there is a specific age at which you will attain FRA. Your FRA is dictated by your year of birth and is the age at which you can begin receiving your full monthly benefit. Your FRA is important because it is half of the equation used to calculate your Social Security benefit. The other half of the equation is based on when you start taking benefits.

When Social Security was initially set up, the FRA was age 65, and it still is for people born before 1938. But as time has passed, the age for receiving full retirement benefits has increased. If you were born between 1938 and 1960, your full retirement age is somewhere on a sliding scale between 65 and 67. Anyone born in 1960 or later will now have to wait until age 67 for full benefits. Increasing the FRA has helped the government reduce the cost of the Social Security program, which paid out almost $870 billion to beneficiaries in 2015!*

While you can begin collecting benefits as early as age 62, the amount you receive as a monthly benefit will be less than it would be if you wait until you reach or surpass your FRA. It is important to note that if you file for your Social Security benefit before your FRA, *the reduction to your monthly benefit will remain in place for the rest of your life.* You can also delay receiving benefits up to age 70, in which case your benefits will be higher than your PIA for the rest of your life.

- At FRA, 100 percent of PIA is available as a monthly benefit.
- At age 62, your Social Security retirement benefits are available. For each month you take benefits prior to your FRA, however, the monthly amount of your benefit is reduced. *This reduction stays in place for the rest of your life.*
- At age 70, your monthly benefit reaches its maximum. After you turn age 70, your monthly benefit will no longer increase.

| Year of Birth | Full Retirement Age |
|---|---|
| 1943-1954 | 66 |
| 1955 | 66 and 2 months |
| 1956 | 66 and 4 months |
| 1957 | 66 and 6 months |
| 1958 | 66 and 8 months |
| 1959 | 66 and 10 months |
| 1960 or later | age 67** |

---

* *https://www.ssa.gov/news/press/basicfact.html*
** *http://www.ssa.gov/OACT/progdata/nra.html*

## ROLLING UP YOUR SOCIAL SECURITY

Your Social Security income "rolls up" the longer you wait to claim it. Your monthly benefit will continue to increase until you turn 70 years old. Even though Social Security is the foundation of most people's retirement, many Americans feel that they don't have control over how or when they receive their benefits. The truth is that every dollar you increase your Social Security income by means less money you will have to spend from your nest egg to meet your retirement income needs, but many retirees do not take advantage of this fact. For many people, creating their Social Security strategy is the most important decision they can make to positively impact their retirement. *The difference between the best and worst Social Security decision can be tens of thousands of dollars over a lifetime of benefits.*

**Deciding NOW or LATER:** Following the above logic, it makes sense to wait as long as you can to begin receiving your Social Security benefit. However, the answer isn't always that simple. Not everyone has the option of waiting. Many people need to rely on Social Security on day one of their retirement. Some might need the income. Others might be in poor health and don't feel they will live long enough to make waiting until their FRA worthwhile for themselves or their families. It is also possible, however, that the majority of folks taking an early benefit at age 62 are simply under-informed about Social Security. Perhaps they make this major decision based on rumors and emotion.

**File Immediately if You:**
- Find your job is unbearable.
- Are willing to sacrifice retirement income.
- Are not healthy and need a reliable source of income.

**Consider Delaying Your Benefit if You:**
- Want to maximize your retirement income.

- Want to increase retirement benefits for your spouse.
- Are still working and like it.
- Are healthy and willing / able to wait to file.

So if you decide to wait, how long should you wait? Lots of people can put it off for a few years, but not everyone can wait until they are 70 years old. Your individual circumstances may be able to help you determine when you should begin taking Social Security. If you do the math, you will quickly see that between ages 62 and 70, there are 96 months in which you can file for your Social Security benefit. If you take into account those 96 months and the 96 months your spouse could also file for Social Security, and the number of different strategies for structuring your benefit, you can easily end up with more than 20,000 different scenarios. It's safe to say this isn't the kind of math that most people can easily handle. Each month would result in a different benefit amount. The longer you wait, the higher your monthly benefit amount becomes. Each month you wait, however, is one less month that you receive a Social Security check.

*The goal is to maximize your lifetime benefits.* That may not always mean waiting until you can get the largest monthly payment. Taking the bigger picture into account, you want to find out how to get the most money out of Social Security over the number of years that you draw from it. Don't underestimate the power of optimizing your benefit: the difference between the BEST and WORST Social Security election can easily be worth thousands of dollars in lifetime benefits. *The difference can be very substantial!*

If you know that every month you wait, your Social Security benefit goes up a little bit, and you also know that every month you wait, you receive one less benefit check, how do you determine where the sweet spot is that maximizes your benefits over your lifetime? Financial professionals have access to software that will calculate the best year and month for you to file for benefits based on your default life expectancy. You can further customize that information by estimating your life expectancy based on your health, habits and family history. If you can then create an income plan (we'll get into this later in the chapter) that helps you wait until the target date for you to file for Social Security, you can optimize your retirement income strategy to get the most out of your Social Security benefit. How can you calculate your life expectancy? Well, you don't know exactly how long you'll live, but you have a better idea than the government does. They rely on averages to make their calculations. *You have much more personal information about your health, lifestyle and family history than they do.* You can use that knowledge to game the system and beat all the other people who are making uninformed decisions by filing early for Social Security.

While you can and should educate yourself about how Social Security works, the reality is you don't need to know a lot of general information about Social Security in order to make choices about your retirement. What you do need to know is exactly *what to do to maximize your benefit.* Because knowing what you need to do has huge impacts on your retirement! For most Americans, Social Security is the foundation of income planning for retirement. Social Security benefits represent about 39 percent of the income of the elderly.* For many people, it can represent the largest portion of their retirement income. Not treating your Social Security benefit as an asset and investment tool can lead to sub-optimization of your largest source of retirement income.

Let's take a look at an example that shows the impact of working with a financial professional to optimize Social Security benefits:

---

* *http://www.socialsecurity.gov/pressoffice/basicfact.htm*

» *Wes and Pam Haymaker are a typical American couple who have worked their whole lives and saved when they could. Wes is 60 years old, and Pam is 56 years old. They sat down with a financial professional who logged onto the Social Security website to look up their PIAs. Wes' PIA is $1,900 and Pam's is $900.*

*If the Haymakers cash in at age 62 and begin taking retirement benefits from Social Security, they will receive an estimated $568,600 in lifetime benefits. That may seem like a lot, but if you divide that amount over 20 years, it averages out to around $28,400 per year. The Haymakers are accustomed to a more significant annual income than that. To make up the difference, they will have to rely on alternative retirement income options. They will basically have to depend on a bigger nest egg to provide them with the income they need.*

*If they wait until their FRA, they will increase their lifetime benefits to an estimated $609,000. This option allows them to achieve their Primary Insurance Amount, which will provide them a $34,200 annual income.*

*After learning the Haymakers' needs and using software to calculate the most optimal time to begin drawing benefits, the Haymakers' financial professional determined that the best option for them drastically increases their potential lifetime benefits to $649,000!*

*By using strategies that their financial professional recommended, they increased their potential lifetime benefits by as much as* ***$80,000.*** *There's no telling how much you could miss out on from your Social Security if you don't take time to create a strategy that calculates your maximum benefit. For the Haymakers, the value of maximizing their benefits was the difference between night and day. While this may seem like a special case, it isn't uncommon to find benefit increases* *of this magnitude. You'll never know unless you take a look at your own options.*

Despite the importance of knowing when and how to take your Social Security benefit, many of today's retirees and pre-retirees may know little about the mechanics of Social Security and how they can maximize their benefit.

So, to whom should you turn for advice when making this complex decision? Before you pick up the phone and call Uncle Sam, you should know that the Social Security Administration (SSA) representatives are actually prohibited from giving you election advice! Plus, SSA representatives in general are trained to focus on monthly benefit amounts, not the lifetime income for a family.

## MAXIMIZING YOUR LIFETIME BENEFIT

As discussed in Chapter 2, calculating how to maximize **lifetime benefits** is more important than waiting until age 70 for your maximum **monthly benefit amount.** It's about getting the most income during your lifetime. Professional benefit maximization software can target the year and month that it is most beneficial for you to file based on your life expectancy.

The three most common ages that people associate with retirement benefits are 62 (Earliest Eligible Age), 66 (Full Retirement Age), and 70 (age at which monthly maximum benefit is reached). In almost all circumstances, however, none of those three most common ages will give you the maximum lifetime benefit.

Remember, every month you wait to file, the amount of your benefit check goes up, but you also get one less check. You don't know exactly how long you're going to live, but you have a better idea of your life expectancy than the actuaries at the Social Security Administration who can only work with averages. They can't make calculations based on your specific situation. A professional can run the numbers for you and get the target date that maximizes your potential lifetime benefits. You can't get this information from the SSA, but you *can* get it from a financial professional.

**Types of Social Security Benefits:**
- *Retired Worker Benefit.* This is the benefit with which most people are familiar. The Retired Worker Benefit is what most people are talking about when they refer to Social Security. It is your benefit based on your earnings and the amount that you have paid into the system over the span of your career.
- *Spousal Benefit.* This is available to the spouse of someone who is eligible for Retired Worker Benefits.
- *Survivorship Benefit.* When one spouse passes away, the survivor is able to receive the larger of the two benefit amounts.
- *Restricted Application.* A higher-earning spouse may be able to start collecting a spousal benefit on the lower-earning spouse's benefit while allowing his or her benefit to continue to grow. Due to the Bipartisan Budget Act of 2015, this option is only available to individuals who turned age 62 before January 1, 2016.

In November of 2015, the Bipartisan Budget Act of 2015 was passed, which will have a dramatic impact on the way many Americans plan for Social Security. As the largest change to Social Security since 2000, the Bipartisan Budget Act of 2015 eliminated an estimated $9.5 billion* of benefits to retirees and may

---

* *http://www.nasdaq.com/article/congress-planning-to-close-social-security-loopholes-cm536252*

limit some of the flexibility you previously had to structure your benefits.

In 2000, Congress passed the Senior Citizens Freedom to Work Act. The bill allowed retirees to suspend receiving benefits so they wouldn't be subject to additional taxation if they chose to return to work after they filed for Social Security. However, by doing so, the bill also unintentionally created several loopholes in claiming strategies: most notably, the Restricted Application for spousal benefits and "file and suspend" filing strategy. For most Americans, the Bipartisan Budget Act of 2015 closed these loopholes by eliminating "file and suspend" and the Restricted Application.

The new rules mandate that:

- If a primary worker is not currently receiving benefits, then their dependents (child, spouse) can no longer collect benefits based on the primary worker's earning record.
- If you file for benefits, then you are filing for *all* benefits to which you are entitled—not just the benefit type you choose.

It's important to remember that in spite of these immense changes, one thing stayed the same—filing for Social Security is one of the most important financial decisions you will make in your lifetime, and a financial professional can help ensure you make the right one.

## THE DIVORCE FACTOR

How does a divorced spouse qualify for benefits? If you have gone through a divorce, it might affect the retirement benefit to which you are entitled.

In general, a person can receive benefits as a divorced spouse on a former spouse's Social Security record so long as the following conditions are met:

- the marriage lasted at least 10 years; and
- the person filing for divorce benefits is at least age 62, unmarried, and not entitled to a higher Social Security benefit on his or her own record.*

With all of the different options, strategies and benefits to choose from, you can see why filing for Social Security is more complicated than just mailing in the paperwork. Gathering the data and making yourself aware of all your different options isn't enough to know exactly what to do, however. On the one hand, you can knock yourself out trying to figure out which options are best for you and wondering if you made the best decision. On the other hand, you can work with a financial professional who uses customized software that takes all the variables of your specific situation into account and calculates your best option. You have tens of thousands of different options for filing for your Social Security benefit. If your spouse is a different age than you are, it nearly doubles the amount of options you have. This is far more complicated arithmetic than most people can do on their own. If you want a truly accurate understanding of when and how to file, you need someone who will ask you the right questions about your situation, someone who has access to specialized software that can crunch the numbers. The reality is that you need to work with a professional that can provide you with the sophisticated analysis of your situation that will help you make a truly informed decision.

**Important Questions about Your Social Security Benefit:**
- *How can I maximize my lifetime benefit?* By knowing when and how to file for Social Security. This usually means waiting until you have at least reached your Full Retire-

---

* *http://www.ssa.gov/retire2/yourdivspouse.htm*

ment Age. A professional has the experience and the tools to help determine when and how you can maximize your lifetime benefits.

- *Who will provide reliable advice for making these decisions?* Only a professional has the tools and experience to provide you reliable advice.
- *Will the Social Security Administration provide me with the advice?* The Social Security Administration cannot provide you with advice or strategies for claiming your benefit. They can give you information about your monthly benefit, but that's it. They also don't have the tools to tell you what your specific best option is. They can accurately answer how the system works, but they can't advise you on what decision to make as to how and when to file for benefits.

The Maximization Report that your financial professional will generate represents an invaluable resource for understanding how and when to file for your Social Security benefit. When you get your customized Social Security Maximization Report, you will not only know all the options available to you—but you will understand the financial implications of each choice. In addition to the analysis, you will also get a report that shows *exactly* at what age—including which month and year—you should trigger benefits and how you should apply. It also includes a variety of other time-specific recommendations, such as when to apply for Medicare or take Required Minimum Distributions from your qualified plans. A report means there is no need to wonder, or to try to figure out when to take action—the Social Security Maximization Report lays it all out for you in plain English.

## CHAPTER 5 QUICK TIPS //

- Social Security is not only one of the best annuities that money can buy, but it is one of the largest retirement assets that you have at your disposal. Be smart: before you make the decision to turn on your Social Security benefit, ask your financial professional for a Social Security Maximization report. You only get one shot at getting it right!
- When it is time to file for benefits, consider filing online. It's been our experience that the staff people who call back typically tend to be a little savvier than those working on the front lines at the administration's office.

# 6

# HOW TO CREATE CASH FLOW FOR LIFE

*In retirement, financial peace of mind doesn't come from a pile of money that could potentially run out, but rather it comes from guaranteed cash flow, a paycheck for life!*

The moment that you stop working and start living off the money that you've set aside for retirement can be referred to as the **Retirement Cliff**. You've worked and earned money your whole life, but the day that you retire, that income comes to an end. That's the day that you start relying on other assets that can be used to provide the income.

If your monthly Social Security check and your other supplemental income leave a shortfall in your *desired* income, how are you going to fix it? This shortfall is called the **Income Gap** and it needs to be filled in order to maintain your lifestyle into retirement. You basically want to buy that income gap for the least amount of money possible. You don't want it to cost you too much, because you want to get the most out of your other assets, including planning for your future and planning for your legacy.

If you could have the option to contribute more money toward Social Security in order to secure more guaranteed income, it would be a great way to create a Green Money asset that would enhance your retirement. Since that option isn't available, you may seek an investment tool that is similar to Social Security that provides you with a reliable income.

In retirement, financial peace of mind doesn't come from a pile of money that could potentially run out, but rather it comes from having a guaranteed cash flow, a paycheck for life! With this element added to your portfolio, you can sleep well at night knowing that your income is secure and that you never have to worry about another 2008 robbing you of this part of your nest egg and the guaranteed income stream that it generates.

## WHAT FLAVOR DO YOU NEED?
### IRREVOCABLE VS REVOCABLE

Back in the day when people relied on traditional pensions, companies relied on the strength of insurance companies to pay out those steady incomes. Today, retirees are in charge of creating their own income streams, but you can still rely on the strength of insurance companies to create your own private pension for your core income needs.

Annuities come in different flavors. Like ice cream, you can also have a lot of mix-ins or special toppings. Just as the two main flavors of ice cream are chocolate and vanilla, the two main kinds of annuities can be divided into the categories of **Irrevocable** and **Revocable**. Part of the reason why people hear so many contrasting opinions about these products is because most people don't understand how different annuities can be from one another. Let's take a look at which annuities might appeal to your palate.

**IRREVOCABLE ANNUITIES:** These annuities are a simple contract between you and an insurance company where you give a lump sum of money in exchange for a guaranteed income over an agreed-upon time period. That time period could be five years, or it could be for the remainder of your lifetime. In exchange for this reliable income, you give up lump-sum access to your funds, which is why we call this type of annuity *irrevocable*. When you pass away, the income stops unless you have added another option on it. Once you elect your options and the income starts, you can't go back and change it or access the money in your account except as an income payment. Guarantees from insurance companies are based on the claims-paying ability of the issuing insurance company.

One of the most common types of irrevocable annuities is the single premium immediate annuity, also known as the SPIA. SPIAs provide investors with a stream of reliable income when they can't afford to take the risk of losing money in a fluctuating market. If you want to provide for a spouse in the event of your passing, you will want to ask your financial professional about your options for doing so with a SPIA. SPIAs offer benefits that can provide for a joint-for-life income for married persons. Your financial professional can walk you through a series of different payment options to help you select the one that most closely fits your needs. If you are looking for an income creation tool that has a bit more flexibility to it, today's newer revocable annuities might be more to your liking.

**REVOCABLE ANNUITIES:** These newer types of annuities give you a place to put your money where you can turn on an income stream for yourself or your spouse, have access to the cash value, and when you pass away, any amount left in the account goes to your beneficiaries.

There are three main kinds of revocable annuities, and not all of them are a Green Money investment, which often creates confusion. Here is what you need to know before you order-up an annuity to satisfy your appetite:

**The Fixed Annuity**: A fixed annuity will pay you out an income based on a guaranteed fixed rate of return. In today's market, fixed annuities are paying anywhere from 2 to 3 percent. If the market hits an all-time high of 26 percent, you get 3 percent. If the market takes a deadly drop of 40 percent, *you still get that 3 percent.* This is a safe, Green Money investment. You can't lose your principal with a fixed annuity and you are guaranteed a set rate of return.

**The Variable Annuity:** As their name suggests, variable annuities vary with the market and are a Red Money investment. They do NOT offer a guarantee of your principal but rather offer direct participation in the stock market.

Because variable annuities are invested in mutual funds, there are management fees assessed for each fund in addition to the other expense fees, making the variable annuity one of the more expensive investments that you can own. Here is what financial advisor, author, and television host Suze Orman has to say about variable annuities on page 504 of her book "The Road to Wealth": "For many reasons including high fees and benefits that, in my opinion, are overstated by sales people, variable annuities are an investment I often warn against." If you suspect you might have a variable annuity, ask a fiduciary professional to examine your contract and make recommendations that are in your best interest.

**The Fixed Indexed Annuity:** The Fixed Indexed Annuity (FIA) is the newest flavor to the annuity scene. It is sometimes called a hybrid annuity because it borrows elements from both the fixed and variable annuities mentioned above. From the fixed annuity, the FIA gets its Green Money guarantees to ensure your principal is safe. But what about market gains? This is where the word index comes into play. The FIA is able to credit interest based on market gains without the unpredictability of market loss.

What does Suze Orman have to say about the indexed annuity? On pages 511 and 513 respectively of "The Road to Wealth" she writes: "It was created to compete with very popular index funds, mutual funds that track a stock market index. I have to admit I like the concept." Later, she adds: "If you do not want to take any risk but still want to play the stock market, a good indexed annuity may be right for you."

The rest of this chapter is devoted to the features and benefits of this newer, hybrid annuity so you can determine if an indexed option might be a good addition to your portfolio.

## THE HYBRID APPROACH TO YOUR INCOME NEEDS

Today, you probably have savings in a variety of assets that you acquired over the years. But you may not have taken time to examine them and assess how they will support your retirement. **It's not about IF the market goes up or down, but WHEN it does.** If it goes down at the wrong time for your five or 10 year retirement horizon, you could be in serious danger of losing some or outliving your money. **Ask yourself the following questions:**

- How concerned are you about finding a secure financial vehicle to protect your savings?
- How concerned are you about having a steady stream of cash flowing into your bank account?

If you are searching for the best way to fill your income gap, a fixed indexed annuity investment tool is likely a good option for you. In fact these annuities have many similar qualities to Social Security that give them the same look and feel as that reliable benefit check you get every month. Most importantly, a fixed indexed annuity can be an efficient and profitable way to solve your income gap.

Let's say you have saved $100,000 and need it to generate income to meet your needs above and beyond your Social Security and pension checks. You give the $100,000 to an insurance company, who in turn invests it to generate growth. When you use that $100,000 to buy a fixed indexed annuity, you are pegging your money on an index. It could be the S&P 500, the Dow Jones Industrial Average or any number of indexes.

The following story illustrates how using an indexed and fixed annuity can fill your income gap and save you money:

> » *Makenzie is 60 years old and is wondering how she can use her assets to provide her with a retirement income. She has a $5,000 per month income need. If she starts withdrawing her Social Security benefit in six years at age 66, it will provide her with $2,200 per month. She also has a pension that kicks in at age 70 that will give her another $1,320 per month.*
>
> *That leaves an income gap of $2,800 from ages 66 to 69, and then an income gap of $1,480 at age 70 and beyond. If Makenzie uses only Green Money to solve her income need, she will need to deposit $918,360 at 2 percent interest to meet her monthly goal for her lifetime. If she opts to use Red Money and withdraws the amount she needs each month from the market, let's say the S & P 500, she will run out of cash in 10 years if she invested between the years of 2000 and 2012. Suffering a market downturn like that during the period for which she is relying on it for retirement income will change her life, and not for the better.*
>
> *Working with a financial professional to find a better way, Makenzie found that she could take a hybrid approach to fill her income gap. Her professional recommended two different income vehicles: one that allowed her to deposit just $190,161 with a 2 percent return, and one that was a $146,000 fixed indexed annuity. These tools filled her income*

*gap with $336,161, requiring her to spend $582,000 less money to accomplish her goal! Working with a professional to find the right tools for her retirement needs saved Makenzie over half a million dollars.*

## DO YOU NEED AN INCOME RIDER?

Up to this point, the indexed annuity is a "no fee" investment. They are making their money on the "spread" just like the bank does with a CD. However, to generate income from the annuity, you select something called an income rider. You might think of an income rider as the whipped cream, sprinkles, and cherry on your annuity. Just like you can't make a sundae without these ingredients, you can't get a guaranteed lifetime income stream from a **revocable annuity** unless you add the income rider. If your goal is to create a lifetime guaranteed income stream for you or for both you and your spouse, either immediately or sometime in the future, you may want to consider adding on an income rider.

How do these income riders work? Essentially, they create a separate account from which the insurance company will pay you an income while you have your money in their annuity. Your income rider is a larger number than what your investment is actually worth, and if you select the income rider, it will increase in value over time, providing you with more income. As the insurance company holds your money and invests it, they generate a return on it that they use to pay you a regular monthly income based on a higher number.

When you opt for an income rider, an insurance company can reliably predict how much money they will pay out to you over a set period of time. It's predictable and insurance companies like that. They can base their business on those predictable numbers.

## THE POWER OF ANNUAL RESET

One of the most attractive features of income riders is something called annual reset. Annual reset is sometimes also referred to as a "ratcheting." Instead of taking on the risk that comes with putting money in a fluctuating market, you can offset that risk onto the insurance company. It works like this: **If the market goes down, you don't suffer a loss.** Instead, the insurance company absorbs it. But if the market goes up, you share with the insurance company some of the profit made on the gain.

The graph you see here illustrates how the annual reset feature of a fixed indexed annuity (FIA) with an income rider can work for you:

**The line at the bottom** is the historical performance of the S&P 500 from 1999 to 2015. If you started with $100,000 on the 31st of December, 1999, and rode the roller coaster and held on the entire time, you would have ended up with $139,115 by the end of December, 2015.

**The middle line** is a hypothetical example of how a fixed indexed annuity might have performed during the same time period. The money placed in an FIA has a contractual guarantee of principal, is never directly invested into the market, and will not be affected by negative market performance. For example, when the market lost roughly 40 percent of its value by the end of 2002, the account value of the annuity remained at $100,000.

**The line at the top** represents how an Income Rider would work. Although it is possible to find an FIA that does not charge a rider fee, most will come with one. By adding the income rider, the income account value will grow at a specified, guaranteed rate each year you defer turning on the income stream—and this guarantee is regardless of index performance.

**What's important to know about the income account value is that it is NOT a value that you can cash out.** It's a value that your lifetime income payments are based upon. In the example

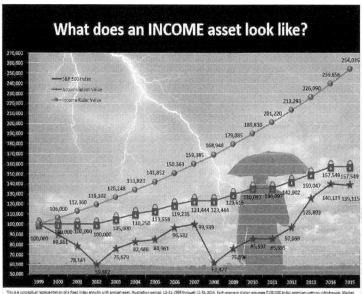

above, the 2015 income account value is $254,035. That means if you decided to turn on the lifetime income and the payout factor at your current age was 5 percent, then you would receive $12,701 for the rest of your life. When you passed away, your beneficiaries would (in most cases) receive whatever was left in your actual account value, represented by the middle line. If you wanted to withdraw money, it would come from the account value—or the middle line—and not the top line or income account value.

Remember: the FIA is only credited **a portion** of the index gains and this is what makes this vehicle *not* too good to be true! Notice that when the market began to rebound and earned a positive return in 2013, the account value of the FIA (the middle line) grew as well, but it didn't get all of the returns. The FIA grows by earning interest credits based upon positive performance of the index. The amount of gain you get is called your annuity participation rate. Typically the insurer will cap the amount of gain you can realize at somewhere between 3 and 7 percent. If the market goes up 10 percent, you would realize a portion of that gain (whatever percentage you are capped at). This means you never lose money on your investment, while always gaining a portion of the upswings. The measurement period of your annuity can be calculated monthly, weekly and even daily, but most annuities are measured annually.

So, as the market continued to grow from 2003 to 2007, the FIA participated in that positive performance of the index each year. When 2008 hit and the market plummeted by 38 percent, what happened to the account value of the FIA? That's right, nothing. It remained at the same value as it was at the end of the previous year. So you get the picture: the FIA is linked to an outside index. In the years that the index has positive performance, the FIA participates in that performance by receiving indexed interest, but it is only credited a portion of the index gains.

These days there are many different crediting strategies available within each annuity, from a fixed interest rate to a relatively new "uncapped" interest crediting strategy. Your advisor can help you determine the best allocation for the choices you have available. No investment can get you all of the gains all of the time, but you CAN get an income based on guarantees. So think about the realities of the stock market and ask yourself, what would you rather have your income payments based on?

The following example shows just how helpful an indexed annuity option with an income rider can be for a retiree:

> » *Jerry and Denise are 62 years old and have decided to run the numbers to see what their retirement is going to look like. They know they currently need $6,000 per month to pay their bills and maintain their current lifestyle. They have also done*

*their Social Security homework and have determined that, between the two of them, they will receive $4,200 per month in benefits. They also receive $350 per month in rent from a tenant who lives in a small carriage house in their backyard. Between their Social Security and the monthly rent income, they will be short $1,450 per month.*

*They do have an additional asset, however. They have been contributing for years to an IRA that has reached a value of $350,000. They realize that they have to figure out how to turn the $350,000 in their IRA into $1,450 per month for the rest of their life. At first glance, it may seem like they will have plenty of money. With some quick calculations, they find they have 240 months, or nearly 20 years, of monthly income before they exhaust the account. When you consider income tax, the potential for higher taxes in the future, and market fluctuations (because many IRAs are invested in the market), the amount in the IRA seems to have a little less clout. Every dollar Jerry and Denise take out of the IRA is subject to income tax, and if they leave the remainder in the IRA, they run the risk of losing money in a volatile market. Once they retire and stop getting a paycheck every two weeks, they also stop contributing to their IRA. And when they aren't supplementing its growth with their own money, they are entirely dependent on market growth. That's a scary prospect. They could also withdraw the money from the IRA and put it in a savings account or CD, but removing all the money at once will put them in a tax bracket that will claim a huge portion of the value of the IRA. A seemingly straightforward asset has now become a complicated equation. Jerry and Denise didn't know what to do, so they met with their financial professional.*

*Their financial professional suggested that they use the money to purchase an indexed annuity with an income rider.*

*They selected an annuity that was designed for their specific situation. They took the lump sum from their IRA, placed it in an indexed annuity taking advantage of annual reset so they never lost the value of their investment. In return, they were guaranteed the $1,450 of income per month that they needed to meet their retirement goals. The simplicity of the contract allowed them to do an analysis with their professional just once to understand the product. They basically put their money in an investment crockpot where they didn't have to look at it or manage it. They just needed to let it simmer. In fact, their professional was able to find an annuity for them that allowed them their $1,450 monthly payment with a lump sum of $249,455, leaving them more than $100,000 to reinvest somewhere else. Keep in mind that annuities are tax deferred, meaning you will pay tax on the income you receive from an annuity in the year you receive it.*

## ONE OF THE BEST THINGS ABOUT ANNUITIES: SURRENDER CHARGES

If I were to ask you what is the exact minimum price that you could sell your house for in five years, could you answer that question? What about your favorite stock? If you sold in three years, could you tell me exactly what the minimum amount of cash would be that you walk away with? Of course not. But with a fixed annuity, you know exactly what you could sell it for in every year during the surrender term. What other financial vehicle can do that for you?

In order to encourage investors to leave their money in their annuity contracts, insurance companies create surrender periods that protect their investments. If you remove more than the "penalty free" amount of money (typically 10 percent per year) from the annuity contract during the surrender period or "term" of the annuity, you will pay an early withdrawal or surrender penalty on the excess. A typical surrender period is 10 years. If after three years you decide that you want your $100,000 back, the insurance company has that money tied up in bonds and other investments with the understanding that they will have it for another seven years. Because they will take a hit on removing the money from their investments prematurely, you will have to pay a surrender charge that makes up for their loss on any withdrawal in excess of the penalty free amount. The higher returns that you are guaranteed from an annuity are dependent on the timeframe you selected. The longer an insurance company can hold your money, the easier it is for them to guarantee a predictable return on it.

**If you leave your money in the annuity contract, you get a reliable monthly income no matter what happens in the market.** Once the surrender period has expired, you can move 100 percent of your money whenever you want. Your money becomes totally liquid again because the insurance company has used it in an investment that fit the timeline of your surrender period. For many people, this is an attractive trade off that can provide a creative solution for filling their income gap.

**Additional Annuity Information:**

- One of the most recent innovations with Income Riders is the ability to have the income double in the event of a chronic illness such as a long-term care event. For example, if you are receiving $2,000 a month of guaranteed income from your annuity and you are either confined to a facility or unable to perform two out of six activities of daily living (ADLs), the income would double to $4,000 a month for a period of time to help you meet those extra costs. After the time period, the income would revert back to the original $2,000. This is a long-term care alternative, but not a replacement for traditional long-term care insurance.

- Annuities with income riders are investment tools that look and feel a bit like Social Security. Every year you allow the money to grow with the market, and it will "roll up" by a specific amount, paying out a specific percent to you as income each year.
- Annuities can work very well to create income, and a financial professional can help you find the one that best matches your income need, and can also structure it to work perfectly for you.

When is an annuity with an income rider right for you? A good financial professional can help you make that determination by taking the time to listen closely to your situation and understanding what your needs are as you enter retirement. Every salesperson has a bag full of brochures and PowerPoint presentations, but they need to know exactly what the financial concerns of their individual clients are in order to help them make the most informed and beneficial decision. Some people need income today; others need it in five or 10 years. Taking the time to create a written income plan will better help you determine which kind of annuity and what features are best suited to your individual situation.

## CREATING AN INCOME PLAN

Creating an income plan before you retire allows you to satisfy your need for lifetime income and ensures that your lifestyle can last as long as you do. You also want to create a plan that operates in the most efficient way possible. Doing so will give more security to your Need Later Money and will potentially allow you to build your legacy down the road.

Here is a basic roadmap of what we have covered so far:

- Review your income needs and look specifically at the shortfall you may have during each year of your retirement based on your Social Security income, and income from any other assets you have.

- Ask yourself where you are in your distribution phase. Is retirement one year away? 10 years away? Last year?
- Determine how much money you need and how you need to structure your existing assets to provide for that need.
- If you have an asset from which you need to generate income, consider options offered by purchasing a low-cost revocable annuity such as the Fixed Indexed annuity with an income rider.

## CHAPTER 6 QUICK TIP //

- Like ice cream, annuities come in different flavors. Use them as a piece of the portfolio pie, and make sure you have access to adequate amounts of liquidity.

# 7
# THE TRUTH ABOUT LOSS DURING RETIREMENT

*"There are two rules of investing: Rule #1 – Don't lose money.*
*Rule #2 – Never forget Rule #1."*
*– Warren Buffett*

The above quote mentions the two rules for investing, and this chapter will explain the importance of those rules as it relates to your distribution years. Generally speaking, there are also two kinds of investors that we see coming through our office. There are the do-it-yourself investor types, and those who rely on the big-name firms and work with a broker. The interesting thing is that their results and methods are about the same. They are typically utilizing only buy & hold portfolios. When the markets are up, their accounts are up; when the markets are down, their accounts are down. Both of these methods may have worked just fine during the accumulation phase of your life, because you consistently making ongoing contributions to your accounts. However, as you are preparing to move into this new season of your life, your game plan also needs to change. If you use the same methodologies to get *through* retirement that got you *to* retirement, you run the risk of potentially outliving your money.

## THE BEST AND THE WORST DAYS OF THE MARKET

It can be challenging to watch the stock market's erratic changes every month, week or even every day. When you have your money which represents a lifetime of hard work, saving and investing riding on it, the ride can feel pretty bumpy. When you are managing your money by yourself, emotions inevitably enter into the mix. The Dow Jones Industrial Average and the S&P 500 represent more to you than market fluctuations. They represent a portion of your retirement. It's hard not to be emotional about it.

**Everyone knows you should buy low and sell high, it's common sense, but not common practice. This is what is more likely to happen:**

The market takes a downturn, similar to the 2008 crash, where investors saw the S&P 500 plummet by 55 percent from October 2008 to March 2009. They sit paralyzed as they watch their own accounts lose money, month after month, and their retirement dreams fade away. Everywhere they turn, the advice they hear is, "You can't sell now because if you do, you can never earn back the money that was lost." In fact, many brokers will tell you that it's not a "loss" but only a "paper loss" until you actually sell. I say, "Hog wash!" Once you take a loss, you lose the ability to compound on that money, which means you will need to rely on even larger gains just to get back to where things were before the downturn. At this point most people sell. But eventually, and inevitably, the market begins to rise again. Maybe slowly, maybe with some moderate growth, but by the time the average investor notices an upward trend and wants to buy in again, they have already missed a great deal of the gains.

This is what your broker will point to when trying to convince you of the need to stay in the market. He or she will show you some kind of chart that shows you just how much money you will miss out on gaining if you miss the best days of the market. If they use numbers from Yahoo Finance, they might tell you that from 1990 to the year 2012, the S&P averaged an annual rate of return of 6.18 percent. Using that time frame, your broker might calculate the following for you:

| IF YOU MISSED THESE DAYS: | THEN YOUR AVERAGE RETURN FELL TO: |
|---|---|
| BEST 10 DAYS | 3.02% |
| BEST 20 DAYS | 0.92% |
| BEST 30 DAYS | -0.87% |
| BEST 40 DAYS | -2.52% |

Yikes! With numbers like that, it's no wonder people decide to stay in the market. **A broker looks at the market in terms of keeping you in so you don't miss the best days.** The broker tells you to stay in the market, so you stay, lose money, and then bite off your fingernails while you hope you can earn that money back again. Your gut is telling you to protect what you have left and not to lose more money, but Wall Street, your broker and the financial press are telling you that it's okay, because you are "in it for the long haul."

On the other hand, we have our intrepid investor going it alone, investing without any guidance. The problem with this strategy is two-fold. First, the average investor has no exit strategy, and if they do, it is based on little more than emotion. For those who have established a "risk budget" for their portfolio and actually have a disciplined "exit strategy" to protect their capital, how do they know when to get back in? Most do not have a disciplined and non-emotional strategy for re-entering the market. They miss the best days. Second, they lose even more money by being in the market during the worst days.

DALBAR's "Quantitative Analysis of Investor Behavior" study has been used to measure the effects of investors' buying, selling and mutual fund switching decisions since 1994. The QAIB shows time and time again over nearly a 20 year period that **the average investor earns less,** and in many cases, significantly less than the performance of the actual mutual funds that they hold. Furthermore, the average fixed income investor has failed to keep up with inflation in nine out of the last 14 years.*

Obviously, neither of these methods is an efficient way to be invested in the market during your distribution years. There is a more efficient and effective way for retirees to access market gains. The strategies offered by Yellow Money can give you a way to control your risk.

## THE IMPORTANCE OF NOT LOSING MONEY

Institutional money managers offer a different way of thinking. They traditionally manage money for large institutions, corporations, pension funds and high net worth individuals. Instead of looking at the market in terms of always being fully invested to ensure that they don't miss the best days, they take a different approach. They manage money from a loss mitigation perspective to protect their clients' assets in extremely volatile times or in bear market cycles. Their objective is to capture 70 to 80 percent of an uptrend while avoiding 70 to 80 percent of a down trend. The chart below gives you the other side of the story and reveals the difference it would make if you missed the "worst days" during the same market period as above—the years 1990 to 2012, with the S&P average return rate of 6.18 percent.

---

* 2013 QAIB, Dalbar, March 2013

| IF YOU MISSED THESE DAYS: | THEN YOUR AVERAGE RETURN GREW TO: |
|---|---|
| WORST 10 DAYS | 9.77% |
| WORST 20 DAYS | 12.33% |
| WORST 30 DAYS | 14.55% |
| WORST 40 DAYS | 16.50% |

As you can see, by missing the worst days, your portfolio stands to gain much more than you might lose by missing out on the best days. This Yellow Money approach still puts your investments at risk in the markets, but it is controlled risk. Red Money or traditional "buy & hold" portfolios will not take proactive action to mitigate losses and take your portfolio to safety. Institutional money managers, on the other hand, use computer algorithms and proprietary software to keep you out of the market during the worst days, but they don't stop there. They also develop a re-entry plan specific to the risk tolerance of the individual that allows you to **get back in,** so you can still have the opportunity to capture some of the best days.

Institutional money management is nothing new. This option has largely been out of reach for the average investor because of the high minimum investment amounts ($1,000,000+) and large net worth required to open an institutionally managed account. Today, due to technology, economies of scale and having access to the right custodians, the average investors can access institutional money management with as little as $25,000.

The visual below shows you how missing out on the worst days can outperform the old rules for investing that seek only to keep you in the market for the best days.

**Investor #1** has a $100,000 "buy & hold" portfolio invested with the strategy of always being in the market to capture the highest gains but without any safety net or strategy to protect their money when the market falls. As a result of this strategy, the investor loses 40 percent in one year, but gains 60 percent in another year. Do the math, and you get a portfolio that is averaging a negative 4 percent return and a portfolio balance of $96,000.

**The Importance of NOT LOSING Money**

| Investor #1:<br>$100,000 | Investor #2:<br>$100,000 |
|---|---|
| 40% Loss: $60,000 | 10% Loss: $90,000 |
| 60% Gain: $96,000 | 42% Gain: $127,800 |
| Total Value Down (4%) | Total Value UP 27% |

**Investor #2**, on the other hand, is working with an institutional money manager who is managing money more from a loss mitigation perspective. They are more interested in hitting "singles & doubles" vs. "home runs" & "strikeouts." They believe they can win by not losing big. Investor #2 starts out with the same $100,000 balance. During that first year when the market took a whopping 40 percent hit, this investor only took a 10 percent loss because his money manager got him out of the market when it got too volatile and their technical indicators gave a sell signal. During year two, as the trends reversed and the markets rebounded, Investor #2 missed out on some of the upside before his portfolio manager got a buy signal to go back in. As a result, he only picked up a gain of 42 percent versus the 60 percent Investor #1 captured. Investor #2, however, has a portfolio that is averaging a positive 27 percent with a nice portfolio balance of $127,800, versus the dismal negative 4 percent return earned by Investor #1.

Imagine for moment that you are retired. Every single month, you have to go out to the mailbox and get your check from your investment portfolio to supplement your Social Security benefit and pension. Which investor would you want to be? Investor #1 or Investor #2?

For investors in or near their distribution years, **when** you take the loss is also just as important as **how much** you lose. The retirement Red Zone is the period of time when you are 5 to 10 year away from retirement. Market losses during this period are particularly dangerous and can be detrimental to the long-term success of your retirement. During this time, even a 10 percent loss can have a kind of contagious effect on your portfolio, infecting it with an illness, metaphorically speaking, so that it becomes too weak to sustain you for the long haul. The following story illustrates how devastating being in the market at the wrong time during the early years of retirement can be for a retiree.

> *» Sandra works for Acme Paper Company for 34 years. During her time there, she acquires bonuses and pay raises that often include shares of stock in the company. She also dedicates part of her paycheck every month to a 401(k) that bought Acme stock. By the time she retires, Sandra has $250,000 worth of Acme stock.*
>
> *Although she had contributes to her 401(k) account every month, Sandra doesn't cultivate any other assets that could generate income for her during retirement. Sandra also retires early at age 62 because of her failing health. The commute to work every day was becoming difficult in her weakened condition and she wanted to enjoy the rest of her life in retirement instead of working at Acme.*
>
> *Because she retires early, Sandra fails to maximize her Social Security benefit. While she lives a modest lifestyle, her income needs will still be $3,500 per month. Sandra's*

monthly Social Security check will only cover $1,900, leaving her with a $1,600 income gap. To supplement her Social Security check, Sandra sells $1,600 of her Acme stock each month to meet her income needs. A $250,000 401(k) is nothing to sneeze at, but reducing its value by $1,600 every month will barely last Sandra 10 years. And that's if the market stays neutral or grows modestly. If the market takes a downturn, the money that Sandra relied on to fill her income gap will rapidly diminish. Even if the market starts going up in a couple of years, it will take much larger gains for her to recover the value that she lost.

Unhappily for Sandra, she retired in 2007, just before the major market downturn that lasted for several years. She lost more than 20 percent of the value of her stock. Because Sandra needed to sell her stock to meet her basic income needs, the market price of the stock was secondary to her need for the money. When she needed money, she was forced to sell however many shares she needed to fill her income gap that month. And if she has a financial crisis, involving her need for medical care, for example, she will be forced to sell stock even if the market is low and her shares are nearly worthless.

Sandra realizes that she could have relied on an investment structured to deliver her a regular income while protecting the value of her investment. She could have kept her $250,000 from diminishing while enjoying her lifestyle into retirement regardless of the volatility of the market. Ideally, Sandra would have restructured her 401(k) to reflect the level of risk that she was able to take. In her case, she would have had most of her money in Green Money assets, allowing her to rely on the value of her assets when she needed them.

## THE RETIREMENT RED ZONE

Earlier we talked about why simply following the same rules for accumulating money that got you here can actually hurt you during the distribution phase of your financial life. Whether the market is high or low during your accumulation years doesn't matter as much to you then, because you aren't relying on your portfolio for income. Instead, you are putting money into the portfolio and benefiting from dollar cost averaging. During retirement, however, unless you secure the proper amount of your portfolio in a Green Money investment first, you stand to take more than just a hit when the market goes down. You could run the risk of running out of money!

**The Red Zone is the five to 10 years prior to and just after retiring.** If a significant drop happens to your portfolio while you are in this zone, you lose the ability to compound your money. With a significant chunk of your savings gone, the money isn't able to grow at the same rate. As a pre or post retiree, you simply don't have the time to wait for your portfolio to earn that money back if you are relying on this money for income. Significant expenses like house payments, the unexpected cost of replacing a broken-down car, and medical bills can put people in a position where they need this money. If you need to sell investments to come up with that money, then you don't have the luxury of selling when you *want* to. Instead, you must sell when you *need* to.

That's why loss during retirement isn't just a paper loss. You lose the power of compounding interest and you'll likely lose sleep as well, unless you've taken precautions to secure your income first.

It doesn't take a financial genius to tell you that market volatility is out of your control. When you have a written income plan in place, you don't have to lose sleep. You'll know you have secured your bottom line by protecting enough of your Red Money investments to generate the amount of guaranteed income needed to live the lifestyle you desire. Instead of worrying when the market fluctuates, you can stand by your plan.

You should also review and discuss your investment plan with your financial professional on a regular basis, ensuring he/she is aware of any changes in your goals, financial circumstances, your health or your risk tolerance. When the economy is under stress and the markets are volatile, investors can also feel vulnerable. That vulnerability causes people to tinker with their portfolios in an attempt to outsmart the market. Once you have your provisional income needs covered and are utilizing institutional money managers, you essentially have the best of both worlds: guaranteed income for life and a "safety net" under your investments exposed to market risk. When you put your head on your pillow at night, you can rest easy knowing that your income is secure, and you never have to worry about another 2008 taking 50 percent of what you have.

## CHAPTER 7 QUICK TIP //

- Don't fool around with the money you need to rely on for income during retirement. Secure the money for your provisional income needs first—the money that you need coming in every month regardless of what is happening in the markets—to cover your monthly expenses. Second, consider how having your Red Money investments converted to Yellow Money and managed from a loss mitigation perspective might give you a stronger advantage for protecting and accumulating wealth. Remember—retirement is the time in your life when you need the money the most.

# 8

# YELLOW MONEY:
## INVESTMENT STRATEGIES FOR MORE SECURE GROWTH

*"Offense sells tickets, but defense wins championships."*
*– Legendary Alabama football coach Paul "Bear" Bryant*

Now that you've calculated the Rule of 100, determined how much risk you have and how much you want, and you've determined how much Green Money you need to meet your short-term and mid-term income needs, it's time to look at what you have left. The money you have left after you've calculated your Green Money needs has the potential of becoming Red Money: your stocks, bonds, mutual funds and other investment products that you want to with the markets for future security or legacy goals. You now have the luxury of taking a closer second look at your Red Money to determine how you would like to manage it because your core income needs are secure.

As you read earlier in the key findings of the DALBAR report, the deck is stacked against the individual investor. Remember that the average investor on a fixed income failed to keep pace with inflation in nine of the last 14 years, meaning the inherent risk in managing your Red Money is very real and could have a lasting impact on your assets. So, how much of your Red Money do you invest, and in what kinds of markets, investment products and stocks do you invest? There are a lot of different directions in which you can take your Red Money. One thing is for sure: significant accumulation depends on investing in the market. How you go about doing it is different for everyone. Gathering stocks, bonds and investment funds together in a portfolio without a cohesive strategy behind them could cause you to miss out on the benefits of a more thoughtful and organized approach. The end result is that you may never really understand what your money is doing, where and how it is really invested, and which investment principles are behind the investment products you hold. While you may have goals for each individual piece of your portfolio, it is likely that you don't have a comprehensive plan for your Red Money, which may mean that *you are taking on more risk than you would like, and are getting less return for it than is possible.*

Enter **Yellow Money.** Yellow Money is money that is managed by a professional *with a purpose.* You might say that institutional money managers have a motto: *"You can win by not losing big."*

After your income needs are met and you have assets that you would like to dedicate to accumulation, there are decisions you need to make about how to invest those assets. You can buy stocks, index funds, mutual funds, bonds—you name it—you can invest in it. However, the difference between Red Money and Yellow Money is that Yellow Money has a cohesive strategy behind it that is *implemented by a professional money manager.* This money manager has access and the ability to move into virtually any asset class—including cash or hedging instruments—that can increase in value even when markets fall. When you have your Red Money managed by managers who are focused on loss mitigation rather than chasing high gains, it becomes Yellow Money. Yellow Money is *money that is being managed with a specific purpose, a specific set of focused goals and a specific strategy in mind.* Yellow Money is still at risk but it is *controlled risk.*

It can be helpful to think of Red Money and Yellow Money with this analogy:

If you needed to travel through an unfamiliar city in a foreign country, you could rent a car or perhaps hire a driver. Were you to drive yourself, you would try to gain guidance from perplexing road signs and need to adhere to traffic rules—with no experience or assistance to lean on. It would take longer to get to where you want to go, and the chance of a traffic accident would be higher. If you hired a driver, they would manage your journey. A driver would know the route, how to avoid traffic, and follow the rules of the road.

Red Money is like driving yourself. With Yellow Money, you are still traveling by car, but now you have a professional working on your behalf.

## TAKING A CLOSER LOOK AT YOUR PORTFOLIO

Think about your investment portfolio. Think specifically of what you would consider your Red Money. Do you know what is there? You may have several different investment products like individual mutual funds, bond accounts, stocks, etc. You may have inherited a stock portfolio from a relative, or you might be invested in a bond account offered by the company for which you worked due to your familiarity with them. While you may or may not be managing your investments individually, the reality is that you probably don't have an overall management strategy for all of your investments. Investments that aren't managed are simply Red Money, or money that is at risk in the market.

Harnessing the earning potential of your Red Money relies on more than a collection of stocks and bonds, however. It needs guided management. A good Yellow Money manager uses the knowledge they have about the level of risk with which you are comfortable, what you need or want to use your money for, when you want or need it and how you want to use it. The Yellow Money strategies that they choose for you will still have a certain level of risk, but under the right management, control and process, you have a far better chance of a successful outcome that meets your specific needs.

When you sit down with an investment professional, you can look at all of your assets together. Chances are that you have accumulated a number of different assets over the last 20, 30 or 50 years. You may have a 401(k), an IRA, a Roth IRA, an account of self-directed stocks, a brokerage account, etc. Wherever you put your money, a financial professional will go through your assets and help you determine the level of risk to which you are exposed now and should be exposed in the future.

Here is a typical example of how an investment professional can be helpful to a future retiree with Yellow Money needs:

*» Melissa is 65 years old and wants to retire in two years. She has a 401(k) from her job to which she has contributed for 26 years. She also has some stocks that her late husband managed. Melissa also has $55,000 in a mutual fund that her sister recommended to her five years ago and $30,000 in another mutual fund that she heard about at work. She takes a look at her assets one day and decides that she doesn't understand what they add up to or what kind of retirement they will provide. She decides to meet with an investment professional. Melissa's professional immediately asks her:*
*1. **Does she know exactly where all of her money is?***
*Melissa doesn't know much about all her husband's stocks,*

*which have now become hers. Their value is at $100,000 invested in three large cap companies. Melissa is unsure of the companies and whether she should hold or sell them.*

**2. Does she know what types of assets she owns?** *Yes and no. She knows she had a 401(k) and IRAs, but she is unfamiliar with her husband's self-directed stock portfolio or the type of mutual funds she owns. Furthermore she is unclear as to how to manage the holdings as she nears retirement.*

**3. Does she know the strategies behind each one of the investment products she owns?** *While Melissa knows she had a 401(k), an IRA and mutual fund holdings, she doesn't know how her 401(k) is organized or how to make it more conservative as she nears retirement. She is unsure whether her IRA is a Roth or traditional variety and how to draw income from them? She really does not have specific investment principles guiding her investment decisions, and she doesn't know anything about her husband's individual stocks. One major concern for Melissa is whether her family would be okay if she were not around?*

*After determining Melissa's assets, her financial professional prepares a consolidated report that lays out all of her assets for her to review. Her professional explains each one of them to her. Melissa discovers that although she is two years away from retiring, her 401(k) is organized with an amount of risk with which she is not comfortable. Sixty percent of her 401(k) is at risk, far off the mark if we abide by the Rule of 100. Melissa opts to be more conservative than the Rule of 100 suggests, as she will rely on her 401(k) for most of her immediate income needs after retirement. Melissa's professional also points out several instances of overlap between her mutual funds. Melissa learns that while she is comfortable with one of her mutual funds, she does not agree with the management principles of the other. In the end, Melissa's professional helps her re-organize her 401(k) to secure her more Green Money for retirement income. Her professional also uses her mutual fund and her husband's stock assets to create a growth oriented investment plan that Melissa will rely on for Need Later Money in 15 years when she plans on relocating closer to her children and grandchildren. By creating an overall investment strategy, Melissa is able to meet her targeted goals in retirement. Melissa's financial professional worked closely with her and her tax professional to minimize the tax impact of any asset sales on Melissa's situation.*

Like *Melissa*, you may have several savings vehicles: a 401(k), an IRA to which you regularly contribute some mutual funds to which you make monthly contributions, etc. But what is your *overall investment strategy?* Do you have one in place? Do you want one that will help you meet your retirement goals? Yellow Money looks at *ALL* your accounts and all their different strategies to create a plan that helps them all work together. Your current investment situation may not reflect your wishes. As a matter of fact, it likely doesn't.

You may have a better understanding of your assets than *Melissa* did, but even someone with an investment strategy can benefit from having a financial professional review their portfolio:

> *» Ernie is 69 years old. He retired four years ago. He relied on income from an IRA for three years in order to increase his Social Security benefit. He also made significant investments in 36 different mutual funds. He chose to diversify among the funds by selecting a portion for growth, another for good dividends, another that focused on promising small cap companies and a final portion that work like index funds. All the money that Ernie had in mutual funds he considered Need Later Money that he wanted to rely on in his 80s. After the*

*stock market took a hit in 2008, Ernie lost some confidence in his investments and decided to sit down with a financial professional to see if his portfolio was able to recover.*

*The professional Ernie met with was able to determine what goals he had in mind. Specifically, the financial professional determined what Ernie actually wanted and needed the money for, and when he needed it. His professional also looked inside each of the mutual funds and discovered several instances of overlap. While Ernie had created diversity in his portfolio by selecting funds focused on different goals, he didn't account for overlap in the companies in which the funds were invested. Out of the 36 funds, his professional found that 20 owned nearly identical stock. While most of the companies were good investments, the high instance of overlap did not contribute to the healthy investment diversity that Ernie wanted. Ernie's financial professional also provided him with a report that explained the concentration ratio of his holdings (noting how much of his portfolio was contained within the top 25 stock holdings), the percentage of his portfolio that each company in which he invested in represented (showing the percentage of net assets that each company made up as an overall position in his portfolio) and the portfolio date of his account (showing when the funds in his portfolio were last updated: as funds are required to report updates only twice per year, it was possible that some of his fund reports could be six months old).*

*Ernie's professional consolidated his assets into one investment management strategy. This allowed Ernie's investments to be managed by someone he trusted who knew his specific investment goals and needs. Eliminating redundancy and overlap in his portfolio was easy to do but difficult to detect since Ernie had multiple funds with multiple brokerage firms. Ernie sat down with a professional to see if his mutual funds could perform well, and he left with a consolidated management plan and a money manager that understood him personally. That's Yellow Money at its best.*

## AVOIDING EMOTIONAL INVESTING

There's no way around it; people get emotional about their money. And for good reason. You've spent your life working for it, exchanging your time and talent for it, and making decisions about how to invest it, save it and make it grow. The maintenance of your lifestyle and your plans for retirement all depend on it. The best investment strategies, however, don't rely on emotions. One of Yellow Money's greatest strengths lies in the fact that it is managed by someone who doesn't make decisions about your money under the influence of emotion.

A well-managed investment account meets your goals as a whole, not in individualized and piecemeal ways. Professional money managers do this by creating requirements for each type of investment in which they put your money. We'll call them "screens." Your money manager will run your holdings through the screens they have created to evaluate different types of investment strategies. A professionally managed account will only have holdings that meet the requirements laid out in the overall management plan that was designed to meet your investment goals. The holdings that don't make it through the screens, the ones that don't contribute to your investment goals, are sold and redistributed to investments that your money manager has determined to be appropriate.

Different screens apply to different Yellow Money strategies. For example, if one of your goals is significant growth, which would require taking on more risk alongside the potential for more return, an investment professional would screen for companies that have high rates of revenue and sales growth, high earnings growth, rising profit margins, and innovative products. On the other hand, if you want your portfolio to be used for income, which would call for lower risk and less return, your professional would screen for dividend yield and sector diversification. *Every investor has a different goal, and every goal requires a customized strategy that uses quantitative screens.* A professional will create a portfolio that reflects your investment desires. If some of the current assets you own complement the strategies that your professional recommends, those will likely stay in your portfolio.

Screening your assets removes emotions from the equation. It removes attachment to underperforming or overly risky investments. Professional money managers aren't married to particular stocks or mutual funds for any reason. They go by the numbers and see your portfolio through a lens shaped by your retirement goals. Your professional understands your wants and needs, and creates an investment strategy that takes your life events and future plans into account. It's a thoughtful approach, and it allows you to tap into the tools and resources of a professional who has built a career around successful investing. Managing money is a full-time job and is best left to a professional money manager.

Removing emotions from investing also allows you to be unaffected by the day-to-day volatility of the market. Your financial professional doesn't ask where the market is going to be in a year, three years or a month from now. If you look at the value of the stock market from the beginning of the twentieth century to today, it's going up. Despite the Great Depression, despite the 1987 crash, despite the 2008 market downturn, the market, as a whole, trends up. Remember the major market downturn in 2008 when the market lost 30 percent of its value? Not only did it completely recover, it has far exceeded its 2008 value. Emotional investing led countless people to sell low as the market went down, and buy the same shares back when the market started to recover. That's an expensive way to do business. While you can't afford to lose money that you need in two, three or five years, your Need Later

Money has time to grow. The best way to do so is to make it Yellow.

## CREATING AN INVESTMENT STRATEGY

Just like Melissa and Ernie, chances are that you can benefit from taking a more managed investment approach tailored to your goals. Yellow Money is generally Need Later Money that you want to grow for needs you'll have in at least 10 years. You can work with your financial planner to create investments that meet your needs within different timeframes. You may need to rely on some of your Yellow Money in 10, 15 or 20 years, whether for additional income, a large purchase you plan on making or a vacation. Whatever you want it for, you will need it down the road. A financial professional can help you rescale the risk of your assets as they grow, helping you lock in your profits and secure a source of income you can depend on later.

So what does a Yellow Money account look like? Here's what it *doesn't* look like: a portfolio with 49 small cap mutual funds, a dozen individual stocks and an assortment of bond accounts. A brokerage account with a hodgepodge of investments, even if goal-oriented, is not a professionally managed account. It's still Red Money. Remember, Yellow Money is a managed account that has an overarching investment philosophy that is not focused on chasing high gains. Professional money managers are more interested in singles and doubles versus homeruns and strikeouts. Working with a professional will help you determine how much risk you should take, how to balance your assets so they will meet your goals and how to plan for the big ticket items, like health care expenses, that may be in your future. Yes, Yellow Money is exposed to risk, but it is controlled risk, and by working with a professional, you can manage that risk in a productive way.

## WHY YELLOW MONEY?

If you have met your immediate income needs for retirement, why bother with professionally managing your other assets? The money you have accumulated above and beyond your income needs probably has a greater purpose. It may be for your children or grandchildren. You may want to give money to a charity or organization that you admire. In short, you may want to craft your legacy. It would be advantageous to grow your assets in the best manner possible. A financial professional has built a career around managing money in profitable ways. They are experts under the supervision of the organization that they represent.

Turning to Yellow Money also means that you don't have to burden yourself with the time commitment, the stress, and the cost of determining how to manage your money. Yellow Money can help you better enjoy your retirement. Do you want to sit down in your home office every day and determine how to best allocate your assets, or do you want to be living your life while someone else manages your money for you? When the majority of your Red Money is managed with a specific purpose by a financial professional, you don't have to be worrying about which stocks to buy and sell today or tomorrow.

## SEEKING FINANCIAL ADVICE: STOCK BROKERS VS. INVESTMENT ADVISOR REPRESENTATIVES

Investors basically have access to two types of advice in today's financial world: advice from stock brokers and advice given by investment advisors. Most investors, however, don't know the difference between types of advice and the people from whom they receive advice. Today, there are two primary types of advice offered to investors: advice given by a commission-based registered representative (brokers) and advice given by fee-based Investment Advisor Representatives. Unfortunately, many investors are not aware that a difference exists; nor have they been explained the distinction between the two types of advice. In a survey taken by TD Ameritrade, the top reasons investors choose to work with an independent registered investment advisor are:*

- Registered Investment Advisors are required, as fiduciaries, to offer advice that is in the best interest of clients
- More personalized service and competitive fee structure offered at a Registered Investment Advisor firm
- Dissatisfaction with full commission brokers

The truth is that there is a great deal of difference between stock brokers and investment advisor representatives. For starters, investment advisor representatives are obligated to act in an investor's best interests in every and all aspect of a financial relationship. Confusion continues to exist among investors struggling to find the best financial advice out there and the most credible sources of advice.

Here is some information to help clear up the confusion so you can find good advice from a professional you can trust:

- Investment advisor representatives have the fiduciary duty to act in a client's best interest at all times with every investment decision they make. As of the writing of this book, stock brokers and brokerage firms usually do not act as fiduciaries to their investors and are not obligated to make decisions that are entirely in the best interest of their customers. For example, if you decide you want to invest in precious metals, a stockbroker would likely offer you a precious metals account from their firm instead of one that best fits the investment strategy of your portfolio.
- Investment advisors give their clients a Form ADV describing the methods that the professional uses to do busi-

---

* *2011 Advisor Sentiment Study, commissioned by TD AMERITRADE. TD Ameritrade, Inc.*

ness. An Investment Advisor also obtains client consent regarding any conflicts of interest that could exist with the business of the professional.

- Stock brokers and brokerage firms are not obligated to provide comparable types of disclosure to their customers.

- Whereas stock brokers and firms routinely earn large profits by trading as principal with customers, Investment Advisors cannot trade with clients as principal (except in very limited and specific circumstances).

- Investment Advisors charge a pre-negotiated fee with their clients in advance of any transactions. They cannot earn additional profits or commissions from their customers' investments without prior consent. Registered Investment Advisors are commonly paid an asset-based fee that aligns their interests with those of their clients. Brokerage firms and stock brokers, on the other hand, have much different payment agreements. Their revenues may increase regardless of the performance of their customers' assets.

- Unlike brokerage firms, where investment banking and underwriting are commonplace, Registered Investment Advisors must manage money in the best interests of their customers. Because Registered Investment Advisors charge set fees for their services, their focus is on their client. Brokerage firms may focus on other aspects of the firm that do not contribute to the improvement of their clients' assets.

- Unlike brokers, Registered Investment Advisors do not get commissions from fund or insurance companies for selling their investment products.

Just to drive home the point, here is what a fiduciary duty to a client means for a Registered Investment Advisor. Registered Investment Advisors must:*

- Always act in the best interest of their client and make investment decisions that reflect their goals.
- Identify and monitor securities that are illiquid.
- When appropriate, employ fair market valuation procedures.
- Observe procedures regarding the allocation of investment opportunities, including new issues and the aggregation of orders.
- Have policies regarding affiliated broker-dealers and maintenance of brokerage accounts.
- Disclose all conflicts of interest.
- Have policies on use of brokerage commissions for research.
- Have policies regarding directed brokerage, including step-out trades and payment for order flow.
- Abide by a code of ethics.

## CHAPTER 8 QUICK TIP //

- By converting your Red Money to Yellow Money, you can sleep better knowing that you have your investments under the watchful eye of a manager who is focused on both growing and protecting your money with a loss mitigation plan.

---

* *2011 Advisor Sentiment Study, commissioned by TD AMERITRADE. TD Ameritrade, Inc.*

# 9

## NEW IDEAS FOR INVESTING

Earlier, we discussed how today's investment options require advice that is relevant to today. Traditional, outdated investment strategies are not only ineffective, they can be harmful to the average investor. One of the most traditional ways of thinking about investing is the risk versus reward trade-off. It goes something like this:

- Investment options that are considered safer carry less risk, but also offer the potential for less return.
- Riskier investment options carry the burden of volatility and a greater potential for loss, but they also offer a greater potential for large rewards.

Most professionals move their clients back and forth along this range, shifting between investments that are safer and investments that are structured for growth. Essentially, the old rules of investing dictate that you can either choose relative safety *or* return, but you can't have both.

Updated investment strategies work with the flexibility of liquidity to remake the rules. Here is how:

**There are three dimensions that are inherent in any investment:** *Liquidity,* *Safety,* **and** *Return.* You can maximize any two of these dimensions at the expense of the third. If you choose Safety and Liquidity, this is like keeping your assets in a checking account or savings account. This option delivers a lot of Safety and Liquidity, but at the expense of any Return. On the other hand, if you choose Liquidity and Return, meaning you have the potential for great return and can still reclaim your money whenever you choose, you will likely be exposed to a very high level of risk.

Understanding Liquidity can help you break the old Risk versus Safety trade-off. By identifying assets from which you don't require Liquidity, you can place yourself in a position to potentially profit from relatively safe investments that provide a higher than average rate of return.

Choosing Safety and Return over Liquidity can have significant impacts on the accumulation of your assets. In Randall's case, the paradigm shift from earning and saving to leveraging assets was a costly one.

> » *Randall is a corn and soybean farmer with 1,200 acres of land. He routinely retains somewhere between $40,000 and $80,000 in his checking and savings accounts. If a major piece of equipment fails and needs repair or replacement, Randall will need the money available to pay for the equipment and carry on with farming. If the price of feed for his cattle goes up one year, he will need to compensate for the increased overhead to his farming operation. He isn't a particularly wealthy farmer, but he has little choice but to keep a portion of money on hand in case something comes*

*up and he must access it quickly. Most of his capital is held in livestock in the pasture or crops in the ground tied up for six to eight months of the year. When a major financial need arises, Randall can't just harvest 10 acres of soybeans and use them for payment. He needs to depend heavily on Liquidity in order to be a successful farmer.*

*Old habits die hard, however, and when Randall finally hangs up his overalls and quits farming, he keeps his bank accounts flush with cash, just like in the old days. After selling the farm and the equipment, Randall keeps a huge portion of the profits in Liquid investments because that's what he is familiar with. Unfortunately for Randall, with his pile of money sitting in his checking account, he isn't even keeping pace with inflation. After all his hard work as a farmer, his money is losing value every day because he didn't shift to a paradigm of leveraging his assets to generate income and accumulate value.*

*Almost anything would be a better option for Randall than clinging to Liquidity. He could have done something better to get either more return from his money or more safety, and at the very least would not have lost out to inflation.*

As you can see, choosing Liquidity solely can be a costly option. The sooner you want your money back, the less you can leverage it for Safety or Return. If you have the option of putting your money in a long-term investment, you will be sacrificing Liquidity, but potentially gaining both Safety and Return. Rethinking your approach to money in this way can make a world of difference and can provide you with a structured way to generate income while allowing the value of your asset to grow over time.

**The question is, how much Liquidity do you *really* need?** Think about it. If you haven't sat down and created an income plan for your retirement, your perceived need for Liquidity is a guess. You don't know how much cash you'll need to fill the income gap if you don't know the amount of your Social Security benefit of the total of your other income options. If you *have* determined your income need and have made a plan for filling your income gap, you can partition your assets based on when you will need them. With a plan in place, *you can use the rules of Safety, Liquidity and Return to make sure your retirement is headed in the right direction.*

## CHAPTER 9 QUICK TIP //

- Work with your investment advisors to develop an emergency fund that satisfies your need for access to quick cash in case of emergencies. Keep all you need in liquid accounts to feel comfortable, but don't keep MORE than you need there, because every dollar stored in these types of accounts is 100 percent lazy and taxable.

# 10

# TAXES AND RETIREMENT

*"I am proud to be paying taxes in the United States. The only thing is—I could be just as proud for half the money."*
*– Arthur Godfrey*

Taxes play a starring role in the theater of retirement planning. Everyone is familiar with taxes (you've been paying them your entire working life), but not everyone is familiar with how to make tax planning a part of their retirement strategy.

Taxes are taxes, right? You'll pay them before retirement and you'll pay them during retirement. What's the difference? The truth is that a strategic approach to taxes can help you save money, protect your assets and ensure that your legacy remains intact.

How can a tax form do all that? The answer lies in planning. **Tax planning** and **tax reporting** are two very different things. Most people only *report* their taxes. March rolls around, people pull out their 1040s or use TurboTax to enter their income and taxable assets, and ship it off to Uncle Sam at the IRS. If you use a CPA to report your taxes, you are essentially paying them to record history. You have the option of being proactive with your taxes and to plan for your future by making smart, informed decisions about how taxes affect your overall financial plan. Working with a financial professional who, along with a CPA, makes recommendations about your finances to you, will keep you looking forward instead of in the rearview mirror as you enter retirement.

## TAXES AND RETIREMENT

When you retire, you move from the earning and accumulation phase of your life into the asset distribution phase of your life. For most people, that means relying on Social Security, a 401(k), an IRA, or a pension. Wherever you have put your Green Money for retirement, you are going to start relying on it to provide you with the income that once came as a paycheck. Most of these distributions will be considered income by the IRS and will be taxed as such. There are exceptions to that (not all of your Social Security income is taxed, and income from Roth IRAs is not taxed), but for the most part, your distributions will be subject to income taxes.

Regarding assets that you have in an IRA or a 401(k) plan that uses an IRA, when you reach 70 ½ years of age, you will be required to draw a certain amount of money from your IRA as income each year. That amount depends on your age and the balance in your IRA. The amount that you are required to withdraw as income is called a Required Minimum Distribution (RMD). Why are you required to withdraw money from your own account? Chances are the money in that account has grown over time, and the government wants to collect taxes on that growth. If you have a large balance in an IRA, there's a chance your RMD could increase your income significantly enough to put you into a higher tax bracket, subjecting you to a higher tax rate.

Here's where tax planning can really begin to work strongly in your favor. In the distribution phase of your life, you have a predictable income based on your RMDs, your Social Security benefit and any other income-generating assets you may have. What really impacts you at this stage is how much of that money you keep in your pocket after taxes. Essentially, *you will make more money saving on taxes than you will by making more money.* If you can reduce your tax burden by 30, 20 or even 10 percent, you earn yourself that much more money by not paying it in taxes.

How do you save money on taxes? By having a plan. In this instance, a financial professional can work with the CPAs at their firm to create a **distribution plan** that minimizes your taxes and maximizes your annual net income.

## BUILDING A TAX DIVERSIFIED PORTFOLIO

So far so good: avoid taxes, maximize your net annual income and have a plan for doing it. When people decide to leverage the experience and resources of a financial professional, they may not be thinking of how distribution planning and tax planning will benefit their portfolios. Often more exciting prospects like planning income annuities, investing in the market and structuring investments for growth rule the day. Taxes, however, play a crucial role in retirement planning. Achieving those tax goals requires knowledge of options, foresight and professional guidance.

Finding the path to a good tax plan isn't always a simple task. Every tax return you file is different from the one before it because things constantly change. Your expenses change. Planned or unplanned purchases occur. Health care costs, medical bills, an inheritance, property purchases, reaching an age where your RMD kicks in or travel, any number of things can affect how much income you report and how many deductions you take each year.

Preparing for the ever-changing landscape of your financial life requires a tax-diversified portfolio that can be leveraged to balance the incomes, expenditures and deductions that affect you each year. A financial professional will work with you to answer questions like these:

- What does your tax landscape look like?
- Do you have a tax-diversified portfolio robust enough to adapt to your needs?
- Do you have a diversity of taxable and non-taxable income planned for your retirement?
- Will you be able to maximize your distributions to take advantage of your deductions when you retire?
- Is your portfolio strong enough and tax-diversified enough to adapt to an ever-changing (and usually increasing) tax code?

» *When Ashlynn returns home after a week in the hospital recovering from a knee replacement, the 77-year-old calls her daughter, sister and brother to let them know she is home and feeling well. She also should have called her CPA. Ashlynn's medical expenses for the procedure, her hospital stay, her medications and the ongoing physical therapy she attended amount to more than $50,000.*

*Americans can deduct medical expenses that are more than 10 percent of their Adjusted Gross Income (AGI). Ashlynn's AGI is $60,000 the year of her knee replacement, meaning she is able to deduct $45,500 of her medical bills from her taxes that year.\* Her AGI dictated that she could deduct more*

---

\* *This scenario presumes permanent laws in effect subsequent to 12/31/16* *than 80 percent of her medical expenses that year.* **Ashlynn didn't know this.**

*Had she been working with a financial professional who regularly asked her about any changes in her life, her spending, or her expenses (expected or unexpected), Ashlynn could have saved thousands of dollars. Ashlynn can also file an amendment to her tax return to recoup the overpayment.*

This relatively simple example of how tax planning can save you money is just the tip of the iceberg. No one can be expected to know the entire U.S. tax code. But a professional who is working with a team of CPAs and financial professionals have an advantage over the average taxpayer who must start from square one on their own every year. Have you been taking advantage of all the deductions that are available to you?

## PROACTIVE TAX PLANNING

The implications of proactive tax planning are far reaching, and are larger than many people realize. Remember, doing your taxes in January, February, March or April means you are writing a history book. Planning your taxes in October, November or December means that you are writing the story as it happens. You can look at all the factors that are at play and make decisions that will impact your tax return *before* you file it.

Realizing that tax planning is an aspect of financial planning is an important leap to make. When you incorporate tax planning into your financial planning strategy, it becomes part of the way you maximize your financial potential. Paying less in taxes means you keep more of your money. Simply put, the more money you keep, the more of it you can leverage as an asset. This kind of planning can affect you at any stage of your life. If you are 40 years old, are you contributing the maximum amount to your 401(k) plan? Are you contributing to a Roth IRA? Are you finding ways to structure the savings you are dedicating to your children's education? Do you have life insurance? Taxes and tax planning affects all of these investment tools. Having a relationship with a professional who works with a CPA can help you build a truly comprehensive financial plan that not only works with your investments, but also shapes your assets to find the most efficient ways to prepare for tax time. There may be years that you could benefit from higher distributions because of the tax bracket that you are in, or there could be years you would benefit from taking less. There may be years when you have a lot of deductions and years you have relatively few. **Adapting your distributions to work in concert with your available deductions** is at the heart of smart tax planning. Professional guidance can bring you to the next level of income distribution, allowing you to remain flexible enough to maximize your tax efficiency. And remember, saving money on taxes makes you more money than making money does.

What you have on paper is important: your assets, savings, investments, which are financial expression of your work and time. It's just as important to know how to get it off the paper in a way that keeps most of it in your pocket. Almost anything that involves financial planning also involves taxes. Annuities, investments, IRAs, 401(k)s, 403(b), and many other investment options will have tax implications. Life also has a way of throwing curveballs. Illness, expensive car repair or replacement, or *any event that has a financial impact on your life will likely have a corresponding tax implication* around which you should adapt your financial plan. Tax planning does just that.

**One dollar can end up being less than 25 cents to your heirs.**

*» When Gerald's father passed away, he discovered that he was the beneficiary of his father's $500,000 IRA. Gerald has a wife and a family of four children, and he knew that*

*his father had intended for a large portion of the IRA to go toward funding their college educations.*

*After Gerald's father's estate is distributed, Gerald, who is 50 years old and whose two oldest sons are entering college, liquidates the IRA. By doing so, his taxable income for that year puts him in a 39.6 percent tax bracket, immediately reducing the value of the asset to $302,000. An additional 3.8 percent surtax on net investment income further diminishes the funds to $283,000. Liquidating the IRA in effect subjects much of Gerald's regular income to the surtax, as well. At this point, Gerald will be taxed at 43.4 percent.*

*Gerald's state taxes are an additional 9 percent. Moreover, estate taxes on Gerald's father's assets claim another 22 percent. By the time the IRS is through, Gerald's income from the IRA will be taxed at 75 percent, leaving him with $125,000 of the original $500,000. While it would help contribute to the education of his children, it wouldn't come anywhere near completely paying for it, something the $500,000 could have easily done.*

As the above example makes clear, leaving an asset to your beneficiaries can be more complicated than it may seem. In the case of a traditional IRA, after federal, estate and state taxes, the asset could literally diminish to as little as 25 percent of its value.

How does working with a professional help you make smarter tax decisions with your own finances? Any financial professional worth their salt will be working with a firm that has a team of trained tax professionals, including CPAs, who have an intimate knowledge of the tax code and how to adapt a financial plan to it.

Here's another example of how taxes have major implications on asset management:

*» Bruce and Elaina, a 62-year-old couple, begin working with a financial professional in October. After structuring their assets to reflect their risk tolerance and creating assets that would provide them Green Money income during retirement, they feel good about their situation. They make decisions that allow them to maximize their Social Security benefits, they have plenty of options for filling their income gap, and have begun a safe yet ambitious Yellow Money strategy with their professional. When their professional asks them about their tax plan, they tell him their CPA handled their taxes every year, and did a great job. Their professional says, "I don't mean who does your taxes, I mean, who does your tax planning?" Bruce and Elaina aren't sure how to respond.*

*Their professional brings Bruce and Elaina's financial plan to the firm's CPA and has her run a tax projection for them. A week later their professional calls them with a tax plan for the year that will save them more than $3,000 on their tax return. The couple is shocked. A simple piece of advice from the CPA based on the numbers revealed that if they paid their estimated taxes before the end of the year, they would be able to itemize it as a deduction, allowing them to save thousands of dollars.*

This solution won't work for everyone, and it may not work for *Bruce and Elaina,* every year. That's not the point. By being proactive with their approach to taxes and using the resources made available by their financial professional, they were able to create a tax plan that saved them money.

## ESTATE TAXES

The government doesn't just tax your income from investments while you're alive. They will also dip into your legacy.

While estate taxes aren't as hot of a topic as they were a few years ago, they are still an issue of concern for many people with assets. While taxes may not apply on estates that are less than $5 million, certain states have estate taxes with much lower exclusion ratios. Some are as low as $600,000. Many people may have to pay a state estate tax. One strategy for avoiding those types of taxes is to move assets outside of your estate. That can include gifting them to family or friends, or putting them into an irrevocable trust. Life insurance is another option for protecting your legacy.

## CHAPTER 10 QUICK TIPS //

- Work with your tax professional's or your investment advisor's CPA alliances to find out if you are using your retirement dollars in the most tax-efficient way possible.
- Tax planning is not the same as tax preparation. One looks forward and the other looks backwards.
- Tax planning can directly affect your beneficiaries, costing them or saving them hundreds of thousands of dollars.

# 11

# TAX ALLOCATION

*"As a tax advisor, I have to constantly remind people that the single biggest benefit in the tax code is the tax exemption for life insurance. There's no question that that's the way to keep most if not all of your money protected from taxes forever."*
*– Ed Slott, CPA*

Although the phrase "nothing is certain except for death and taxes" is most famously attributed to Benjamin Franklin, variations of this saying existed even before the country's first taxes were levied, and these words continue to ring true to this day. However, due to recent upheavals in the American financial landscape, this saying might need to be modified to, "nothing is certain except for death and *increasing* taxes."

In the past 10 years alone, the United States has confronted both a debt ceiling and a fiscal cliff, and the federal debt has continued to grow by unprecedented amounts. With the wellbeing of the economy in jeopardy, legislation regarding debt reduction and tax reform has become a hot button issue. Regardless of which legislation has been, or will be, thrown at the American public, the truth of the matter remains the same: the country's current tax revenues cannot cover its obligations.

If the government wants to keep the lights on, it's going to need more income, which not only means that you can count on being taxed, but also on being taxed at an increasing rate.

## DEBT CEILING – CAUSE AND EFFECTS

Since 1960, the debt ceiling has been raised by Congress 78 times. Increasing the debt ceiling is needed because the government keeps maxing out its credit limit, which it has been reliant upon since the beginning of the Industrial Revolution. Essentially, each time the federal government reaches the end of its line of credit; Congress raises the debt ceiling to extend it. This type of poor money management behavior is nothing new for many Americans: many people overuse their credit cards and rack up an impressive amount of debt. However, most people do not have the ability to raise the credit limit on a card once they have maxed it out—unless they can show they have the ability to pay the balance back. The only way to pay a credit line back is by making more money than you're spending. In other words, responsibility and a balanced budget are critical components to repaying a debt.

The federal government keeps finding ways to increase its credit line without also finding ways to proportionally cut its spending. Although some spending cuts have been put in place, they are not large enough to be worthy adversaries of the current debt situation. Consequently, the continual increasing of the debt ceiling has raised more than just the ability of the federal government to go further into debt; it has also raised concerns and fears about the direction in which the economy is heading. As investors' worry about the impact that future investment valuations may have on their personal wealth grows progressively serious, the market continues to swing unpredictably.

The truth of the matter is that raising the debt ceiling is only one part of the equation required to address the country's debt problem—tax reform is the other. If the government wants to try to staunch the flow of its ever-rising debt, then it will need to make more money, and the only way the government makes money is by collecting taxes. Unfortunately, however, the government frequently collects less than it spends: in 2014, the government collected approximately $42 billion less per month than it was spending.*

## DEBT AND EARNINGS

Currently, the national debt is increasing at an unprecedented rate, rising to levels never seen before and threatening serious harm to the economy. In October 2004, the national debt was $7.4 trillion**, and by October 2014 it had climbed to $17.9 trillion***, which means the national debt grew 241.9 percent during this 10-year time period or 8.4 percent annually compounded. Since that time, the national debt growth rate has receded significantly and the national gross domestic product (GDP) has increased: in 2014, the annual debt growth rate had fallen to 4.5 percent and the GDP was approximately $17.5 trillion, up from $12.3 trillion in 2004.

However, even in spite of this progress, the gravity of the situation remains severe. At the end of 2011, the national debt level was 95.3 percent of the GDP. Economists believe that a sustainable economy exists at a maximum level of approximately 80

---

* *Congressional Budget Office projected deficit baseline 2014 - 2024*
** *CBO, An Update to the Budget and Economic Outlook: 2014 - 2024*
*** *US Department of the Treasury's Bureau of the Fiscal Service, www.treasurydirect. gov/NP/debt/current*

percent. On August 26, 2016, the U.S. national debt was 105.13 percent of the GDP.*

The significance of these two numbers lies within the contrast. The national debt is the amount that needs to be repaid; this can be thought of as the government's credit card balance. The GDP represents the market value of all goods and services produced within a country during a given period. In other words, the GDP represents the gross taxable income available to the government. If debts are increasing at a rate greater than the gross income available for taxation, then the only way to make up the difference is to increase the rate at which the gross income is being taxed.

Since 2011, the national deficit's growth rate has experienced a significant downward trend that is continued throughout 2015. Going forward, however, it is predicted that the deficit will once again begin to increase at an unprecedented rate.** Even more concerning is that the disparity between growth in national debt and growth in GDP is projected to continue, which means the amount of money the federal government owes will far outpace its ability to repay it. As anyone who has struggled with debt can tell you, continually borrowing more money than you make can have potentially disastrous consequences.

The increasing disparity between the debt and GDP rates of growth is not the only disconcerting story: national revenue collection rates offer further cause for concern. Since 1970, the average collection of GDP for revenue was approximately 17.3 percent. In 2012, the collection rate was at 14.4 percent, and rose to above 17 percent in 2014. This increase can be explained by several different tax increases that took place in the intervening years, as well as the effects of recent ROTH conversion limitation removals.

---

*Federal Reserve Bank of St Louis Economic Research*
*** CBO, An Update to the Budget and Economic Outlook: 2014 - 2024*

By 2020, it is predicted the revenue rate will rise to be approximately 19.2 percent. When this increase is related to current tax rates, it means that someone currently in the 39.6 percent tax bracket would be pushed into a 44 percent tax bracket. The reality of this projected increase means that additional tax increases are on the horizon, and it would appear that this is going to be a graduated process that may begin as early as next year. Consequently, when the debt ceiling discussions begin again they may be accompanied by a plan to implement additional tax increases over a period of three to five years.

Unfortunately, analysis of the federal government's budget also shows that regardless of revenue collection rates and increased taxes, the deficit will most likely continue to increase, and without additional spending cuts to help bring the budget into balance, tax increases are likely to continue.

## THE END OF AN ERA

From a historical point of view, taxes are extremely low. The last time the U.S. national debt was even close to the same percentage level of GDP as it is today was for several years after the end of World War II. The maximum tax rate at that point, and through the years from 1944 through 1963, averaged 90 percent. Compare that to the maximum rate of 39.6 percent today, and it becomes very clear that there is a disparity of extreme proportion.

Taxes during this historical period were at extreme levels for nearly 20 years, throughout and following this level of debt-to-GDP. A significant point to note about the difference at that time versus where we are today is the economic activity. The period of 1944 through 1963 was in the heart of both the Industrial Revolution and the birth of the baby-boom generation. Today, we are mired in extreme volatility with frequent periods of boom and bust accompanied by the beginning of the greatest retirement wave ever experienced within the U.S. economy.

To contrast these two time periods with respect to the recovery period is almost asinine, as the external pressures from globalization and domestic unfunded liabilities did not exist or were irrelevant factors during the prior period.

To add insult to injury, U.S. domestic unfunded liabilities were estimated to be about $84 trillion in 2012 and that number has only increased through the intervening years*. These liabilities exist outside of the annual budgetary debt discussed above and are due to items such as Social Security, Medicare and government pensions. The most concerning part of this stems from the fact that we are on the cusp of the greatest retirement wave in U.S. history as the baby-boom generation begins retiring and drawing from the unfunded Social Security for which they currently have entitlement. Over the long-run, expenditures related to healthcare programs such as Medicare and Medicaid are projected to grow faster than the economy overall as the population matures.

To put unfunded liabilities into perspective, consider these as off-balance-sheet obligations similar to those of Enron. Although these are not listed as part of the national debt, they must be paid just the same. The difference between Enron and the U.S. unfunded liabilities is that if the U.S. government cannot come up with the funds to pay all these liabilities through revenue generation then they will print the money necessary to pay the debt.

## WHAT DOES THE SOLUTION LOOK LIKE?

Unfortunately, the general public is in a no-win situation for this solution to the problem. Printing money does not bode well for economic growth as this action creates inflationary pressures that devalue the U.S. dollar and make everyone less wealthy. Cutting the entitlements that compose this liability leaves millions

---

* *National Center for Policy Analysis, How Much Does the Federal Government Owe?,* *June 2012*

of people without benefits they have come to expect. The only other option, and one that the government knows all too well, is increased taxes. In fact, according to a Congressional Budget Office paper issued in 2004*, unfunded liabilities are addressed as follows:

*"The term 'unfunded liability' has been used to refer to a gap between the government's projected financial commitment under a particular program and the revenues that are expected to be available to fund that commitment. But no government obligation can be truly considered 'unfunded' because of the U.S. government's sovereign power to tax—which is the ultimate resource to meet its obligations."*

A balanced budget is going to be required at some point and with this will come higher taxes. Given our current position and projected budgets, it is likely that tax increases are coming in the near future. However, although raising taxes is a strategy to raise money, it is not a solution to the government's current and pending fiscal problems.

How do you prepare? Why spend so much time reassuring you that taxes will increase? Because you have an opportunity to take action. Now is the time to prepare for what is to come by structuring countermeasures for the good, the bad, and the ugly of each of these legislative nightmares through tax-advantaged retirement planning.

The truth of the matter is that you make more money by saving on taxes than you do by making more money. The simplistic logic of this statement makes sense when you discover it takes a $1.50 in earnings to put that same dollar, saved in taxes, back in your pocket.** This simple concept becomes extremely valuable to people in retirement and those living on fixed incomes.

---

\* *CBO paper, Measures of the U.S. Government's Fiscal Position Under Current Law, Sept. 2004*

\*\* *Assuming a 33 percent effective tax rate*

As simple as it sounds, it is much more difficult to execute. Most people fail to put together a plan as they near retirement, beginning with a simple cash flow budget. If you have not analyzed your proposed income streams and expenses, you could not possibly have taken the time to position these cash flows and other events into a tax-preferred plan.

Most people will state, "I have a plan" and thus, they do not need any further assistance in this area. The truth in most instances is that many of these people could not show you their plan, and of the few that could, they would not be able to show you how they have executed it. In this regard, they may as well be Richard Nixon saying, "I am not a crook" for as much as they claim, "I have a plan." The truth lies in waiting.

As you approach or begin retirement, you should look at what cash flows you will have. Do you have a pension? How about Social Security? How much additional cash flow are you going to need to draw from your assets to maintain the lifestyle that you desire?

Most people spend their whole lives saving and accumulating wealth but very little time determining a strategy that will distribute this accumulation in ways that will help them to retain it. You need to make sure you have the appropriate diversification of taxable versus non-taxable assets to complement your distribution strategy.

## THE BENEFITS OF DIVERSIFICATION

Heading into retirement, you should be situated within a diversified tax landscape. The point to spending your whole life accumulating wealth is not to see how big the number is on paper, but rather to be an exercise in how much you put in your pocket after removing it from the paper.

To truly understand tax diversification, you must understand what types of money exist and how each of these will be treated during accumulation and, most importantly, during distribution. The following is a brief summary:

1. Free money
2. Tax-advantaged money
3. Tax-deferred money
4. Taxable money
   a. Ordinary income
   b. Capital gains and qualified dividends

## FREE MONEY

Free money is the best kind of money regardless of the tax treatment, because in the end you have more money than you would have otherwise. Many employers will provide contributions toward employee retirement accounts to offer additional employment benefits and inspire employees to save for their own retirement. With this, employers often will offer a matching contribution in which they will contribute up to a certain percentage of an employee's salary, generally three to five percent, to that employee's retirement account when the employee contributes to their retirement account as well. For example, if an employee earns $50,000 annually and contributes three percent ($1,500) to their retirement account annually, the employer will also contribute three percent ($1,500) to the employee's account. That is $1,500 in free money. Take all that you can get!

## TAX-ADVANTAGED MONEY

Tax-advantaged money is the next best thing to free-money. Although you have to earn tax-advantaged money you do not have to give part of it away to Uncle Sam. Tax-advantaged money comes in three basic forms that you can utilize during your lifetime; four if prison inspires your future, but it's not necessary to discuss that option.

One of the most commonly known forms of tax-advantaged money is municipal bonds, which earn and pay interest that could be federally tax-advantaged, state tax-advantaged, or both state and federal tax-advantaged. There are several caveats that should be discussed in regard to the notion of tax-advantaged income from municipal bonds. First, you will notice that tax-advantaged has several flavors from the state and federal perspective. This is because states will generally tax the interest earned on a municipal bond unless the bond is offered from an entity located within that state. This severely limits the availability of completely tax-advantaged municipal bonds and constrains underlying risk and liquidity factors. Second, municipal bond interest gets added back into the equation for determining your modified adjusted gross income (MAGI) for Social Security and could push your income above the thresholds subjecting a portion of your Social Security income to taxation. In effect, if this interest subjects some other income to taxation then this interest is truly being taxed. Last, municipal bond interest may be excluded from the regular federal tax system, but it is included for determining tax under the alternative minimum tax (AMT) system. In its basic form, the AMT system is a separate tax system that applies if the tax computed under AMT exceeds the tax computed under the regular tax system, the difference between these two computations is the alternative minimum tax.

## TAX-FREE MONEY: ROTH IRA

Roth accounts are probably the single greatest tax asset that has come from Congress outside of life insurance and are well known but rarely used. Roth IRAs were first established by the Taxpayer Relief Act of 1997 and were named after Senator William Roth, the chief sponsor of the legislation. A Roth account is simply an account in the form of an individual retirement account or an employer-sponsored retirement account that allows for tax-advantaged growth of earnings and, thus, tax-advantaged income.

The main difference between a Roth and a traditional IRA or employer-sponsored plan lies within the timing of the taxation. You're probably very familiar with the typical scenario of putting money away for retirement through an employer plan, whereby your employer deducts money from each paycheck and puts it directly into a retirement account. This money is taken out before taxes are calculated meaning you do not pay tax on those earnings today. A Roth account, on the other hand, takes the money *after* the taxes have been taken out and then puts it into the retirement account, so you do pay tax on the money today. The other significant difference between these two is taxation during distribution in later years. With a traditional retirement account, when you take the money out later it gets added to your ordinary income and is taxed accordingly. Additionally, including this in your income subjects you to the consequences previously mentioned for municipal bonds with Social Security taxation, AMT, as well as higher Medicare premiums. A Roth, on the other hand, has tax-advantaged distributions and does not contribute toward negative impact items such as Social Security taxation, AMT, or Medicare premium increases. It essentially comes back to you without tax and other obligations.

The best way to consider the difference between the two accounts is to look at the life of a farmer. A farmer will buy seed, plant it in the ground, grow the crops, and harvest it later for sale. Typically, the farmer would only pay tax on the crops that have been harvested and sold. But if you were the farmer, would you rather pay tax on $5,000 worth of seed that you plant today or $50,000 worth of harvested crop later? The obvious answer is $5,000 worth of seed today. The truth of the matter is that you are a farmer, except you are planting dollars into your retirement account instead of seeds into the earth.

So why doesn't everyone have a Roth retirement account if things are so simple? There are several reasons, but the single greatest reason has been the constraints on contributions. If you earned over certain thresholds (MAGI over $132,000 single and $194,000 joint for 2016),* you were not eligible to make contributions, and, until 2010, if your modified adjusted gross income (MAGI) was over $100,000 (single or joint) then you could not convert a traditional IRA to a Roth. Outside of these contribution limits, most people save for retirement through their employers and most employers are not offering Roth options within their plans. The reason behind this is because Roth accounts are not that well understood and people have been educated to believe that saving on taxes today is the best possible course of action.

## TAX-FREE MONEY: LIFE INSURANCE

As previously mentioned, the single greatest tax asset that has come from Congress outside of life insurance is the Roth account. Life insurance is the little known or discussed tax asset that holds some of the greatest value for your financial history both during life and upon death, and it is by far the best tax-advantaged device available. Traditionally, life insurance is viewed as a way to protect your loved ones from financial ruin upon your demise and it should be noted that everyone who cares about someone should have life insurance. By purchasing a life insurance policy, your loved ones will be assured a financial windfall from the life insurance company when you die that will help them with your final expenses and carry on their lives without you comfortably. The best part about the life insurance windfall is the fact that nobody will have to pay tax on the money received. This is the single

---

* *https://www.irs.gov/retirement-plans/plan-participant-employee/amount-of-roth-ira-contributions-that-you-can-make-for-2016*

greatest tax-advantaged device available, but it has one downside, you do not get to use it. Only your heirs will.

The little known and discussed part of life insurance is the cash value build-up within whole life and universal life (permanent) policies. Life insurance is not typically seen as an investment vehicle for building wealth and retirement planning, although it should briefly be discussed why this thought process should be re-evaluated. Permanent life insurance is generally misconceived as something that is very expensive for a wealth accumulation vehicle as there are mortality charges (fees for the death benefit) that detract from the returns that are available and further, those returns do not yield as much as the stock market over the long run. This is why many times you will hear the phrase "buy term and invest the rest," where "term" refers to term insurance.

It's important to review the two terms just used in regard to life insurance: term and permanent. Term insurance is what most people are familiar with. You purchase a certain death benefit that will go to your heirs upon your death and this policy will be in effect for a certain number of years, typically 10 to 20 years. The 10 to 20 years is the term of the policy and once you have reached that end you no longer have insurance unless you purchase another policy at that point.

On the other hand, permanent insurance has no term period involved, it is permanent as long as the premiums continue to be paid. Permanent insurance generally has higher premiums than term insurance for the same amount of death benefit coverage, and it is this difference that is referred to when people say "invest the rest" because the pure cost of insurance is roughly the same in both types of policies

Simply speaking, there are significant differences between these two policies that do not get taken into consideration when providing a comparative analysis in the numbers. One item that gets lost in the fray when comparing term and permanent insurance is that term usually expires before death, in fact insurance studies show less than 1 percent of all term policies pay out death benefit claims. The issue arises when the term expires and the desire to have more insurance is still present. A term policy with the same benefit will be much more expensive than the original policy and, many times, life events occur, such as cancer or heart conditions, which makes it impossible to acquire another policy and leaves your loved ones unprotected and tax-advantaged legacy planning out of the equation.

Another aspect and probably the most important piece in consideration of the future of taxation is the fact that permanent insurance has a cash accumulation value. Two aspects stand out with the cash accumulation value. First, as the cash accumulation value increases the death benefit will also increase whereas term insurance is level. Second, this cash accumulation offers value to you during your lifetime rather than just your heirs upon death. The cash accumulation value can be used for tax-advantaged income during your lifetime through policy loans. Most importantly, this tax-advantaged income is available during retirement for distribution planning, all while offering the same typical financial protection to your heirs.

A good analogy for the difference between term life insurance and permanent life insurance renting vs. buying a house. Term insurance is like renting a house which typically cost much less out of pocket to get into but you will never build any equity or own it. Permanent life insurance is like buying a house because although it will cost you more initially to get into it you will build equity, receive tax advantages and one day own "free & clear" with no more payments due.

## TAX-DEFERRED MONEY

Tax-deferred money is the type of money from which most people are familiar, but the idea was also briefly reviewed above.

Tax-deferred money is typically your traditional IRA, employer sponsored retirement plan, or a non-qualified annuity. Essentially, money is put into an investment vehicle that will accumulate in value over time and you do not pay taxes on the earnings that grow in these accounts until it is distributed. Taxes must be paid once the money is distributed and, in addition to the taxes, the same negative consequences exist toward additional taxation and expense in other areas as previously discussed.

## TAXABLE MONEY

Taxable money is everything else and is taxable both today and later, whenever it is received.

Of these four types of money, they really come down to two distinct classifications: taxable and tax-advantaged.

The greatest difference when comparing taxable and tax-advantaged income is a function of how much money you will keep after tax. For help in determining what the differences should be, excluding outside factors such as Social Security taxation and AMT, a tax equivalent yield should be used.

## TAX-FREE IN THE REAL WORLD

To put the tax equivalent yield into perspective, consider the following example:

Bob and Mary are currently retired and in the 25 percent tax bracket living on Social Security and interest from investments. They have a substantial portion of their investments in municipal bonds yielding 6.0 percent, which in today's market is quite comforting. The tax equivalent yield they would need to earn from a taxable investment would be 8.0 percent, a 2.0 percent gap which seems almost impossible given current market volatility. However, something that has never been put into perspective is that the interest from their municipal bonds is subject to taxation on their Social Security benefits* (at 21.25 percent). With this, the yield on their municipal bonds would be 4.725 percent**, and the taxable equivalent yield falls to 6.3 percent leaving a gap of only 1.575 percent.

In the end, most people spend their lives accumulating wealth through the best, if not only vehicle they know, a tax-deferred account. This account is most likely a 401(k) or 403(b) plan offered through your employer and may be supplemented with an IRA that was established at one point or another. As the years go by, people blindly throw money into these accounts in an effort to save for a retirement that they someday hope to reach.

The truth is most people have an age selected for when they would like to retire but spend their lives wondering if they will ever be able to actually quit working. To answer this question, you must understand how much money you will have available to contribute toward your needs. In other words, you need to know what your after-tax income will be during this period.

All else being equal, it would not matter if you put your money into a taxable, tax-deferred, or tax-advantaged account as long as income tax rates never change and outside factors are never an event. The net amount you receive in the end will be the same. Unfortunately, this will never be the case. We already know that taxes will increase in the future, meaning we will likely see higher taxes in retirement than during our peak earning years.

Regardless, saving for retirement in any form is a good thing since it appears from all practical perspectives that future government benefits will be cut and taxes will increase. You have the ability to plan today for efficient tax diversification and maximization of your after-tax dollars during your distribution years.

---

*Assuming each dollar of interest subjects a dollar of Social Security income to taxation at 85 percent*

** *6.0 percent – (6.0 percent -21.25 percent) = 4.725 percent*

## CHAPTER 11 QUICK TIPS //

- The future of U.S. taxation is uncertain. You know what the tax rate and landscape is today, but you don't know what's in store for tomorrow. The only thing you can really count on is the trend of increasing taxation.
- Most people are familiar with tax-deferred methods of retirement savings, such as traditional IRAs. By taking action now, you can prepare for the rise in taxes by restructuring your assets to include the benefits of free and tax-advantaged money.
- Tax-advantaged money is money you earn without having to pay taxes on. One of the most common forms includes municipal bonds, but be aware these come with many state and federal complexities.
- Roth IRAs and permanent life insurance are two other forms of tax-advantaged money that can take advantage of today's lower rate when preparing for tomorrow's retirement.

# 12

# THE BRANDEIS STORY

*Would you rather pay taxes now on the seed, or later on the harvest?*

Louis Brandeis provides one of the best examples illustrating how tax planning works. Brandeis was Associate Justice on the Supreme Court of the United States from 1916 to 1939. Born in Louisville, Kentucky, Brandeis was an intelligent man with a touch of country charm. He described tax planning this way:

*"I live in Alexandria, Virginia. Near the Court Chambers, there is a toll bridge across the Potomac. When in a rush, I pay the dollar toll and get home early. However, I usually drive outside the downtown section of the city and cross the Potomac on a free bridge.*

*The bridge was placed outside the downtown Washington, D.C. area to serve a useful social service—getting drivers to drive the extra mile and help alleviate congestion during the rush hour.*

*If I went over the toll bridge and through the barrier without paying a toll, I would be committing tax evasion.*

*If I drive the extra mile and drive outside the city of Washington to the free bridge, I am using a legitimate, logical and suitable method of tax avoidance, and I am performing a useful social service by doing so.*

*The tragedy is that **few people know that the free bridge exists.**"*

Like Brandeis, most American taxpayers have options when it comes to "crossing the Potomac," so to speak. It's a financial planner's job to tell you what options are available. You can wait until March to file your taxes, at which time you might pay someone to report and pay the government a larger portion of your income. However, you could instead file before the end of the year, work with your financial professional and incorporate a tax plan as part of your overall financial planning strategy. Filing later is like crossing the toll bridge. Tax planning is like crossing the free bridge.

Which would you rather do?

The answer to this question is easy. Most people want to save money and pay less in taxes. What makes this situation really difficult in real life, however, is that the signs along the side of the road that direct us to the free bridge are not that clear. To normal Americans, and to plenty of people who have studied it, the U.S. tax code is easy to get lost in. There are all kinds of rules, exceptions to rules, caveats and conditions that are difficult to understand, or even to know about. What you really need to know is your options and the bottom line impacts of those options.

## ROTH IRA CONVERSIONS

The attractive qualities of Roth IRAs may have prompted you to explore the possibility of moving some of your assets into a Roth account. Another important difference between the accounts is how they treat Required Minimum Distributions (RMDs). When you turn 70 ½ years old, you are required to take a minimum amount of money out of a traditional IRA. This amount is your RMD. It is treated as taxable income. Roth IRAs, however, do not have RMDs, and their distributions are not taxable. Quite a deal, right?

While having a Roth IRA as part of your portfolio is a good idea, converting assets to a Roth IRA can pose some challenges, depending on what kinds of assets you want to transfer.

One common option is the conversion of a traditional IRA to a Roth IRA. You may have heard about converting your IRA to a Roth IRA, but you might not know the full net result on your income. The main difference between the two accounts is that the growth of investments within a traditional IRA is not taxed until income is withdrawn from the account, whereas taxes are charged on contribution amounts to a Roth IRA, not withdrawals. The problem, however, is that when assets are removed from a traditional IRA, even if the assets are being transferred to a Roth IRA account, taxes apply.

There are a lot of reasons to look at Roth conversions. People have a lot of money in IRAs, up to multiple millions of dollars. Even with $500,000, when they turn 70 ½ years old, their RMD is going to be approximately $18,000, and they have to take that out whether they want to or not. It's a tax issue. Essentially, if you will be subject to high RMDs, it could have impacts on how much of your Social Security is taxable, and on your tax bracket.

By paying taxes now instead of later on assets in a Roth IRA, you can realize tax-advantaged growth. This strategy has often been compared to paying taxes on the seed versus on the harvest. Naturally, the amount of seed is much less than the final product it grows, and so tax payers are asked to ponder, would you rather pay taxes now on the seed, or later on the harvest? With a Roth IRA, you pay once and you're done paying. Your heirs are done paying. It's a powerful tool. Here's a simple example to show you how powerful it can be:

*Imagine that you pay to convert a traditional IRA to a Roth. You have decided that you want to put the money in a vehicle that gives you a tax-advantaged income option down the road. If you pay a 25 percent tax on that conversion and the Roth IRA then doubles in value over the next 10 years, you could look at your situation as only having paid 12.5 percent tax.*

The prospect of tax-advantaged income is a tempting one. While you have to pay a conversion tax to transfer your assets, you also have turned taxable income into tax free retirement money that you can let grow as long as you want without being required to withdraw it.

There are options, however, that address this problem. Much like the Brandeis story, there may be a "free bridge" option for many investors.

Your financial professional will likely tell you that it is not a matter of whether or not you should perform a Roth IRA conversion, it is a matter of how much you should convert and when.

Here are some of the things to consider before converting to a Roth IRA:

- If you make a conversion before you retire, you may end up paying higher taxes on the conversion because it is likely that you are in some of your highest earning years, placing you in the highest tax bracket of your life. It is possible that a better strategy would be to wait until after you retire, a time when you may have less taxable income, which would place you in a lower tax bracket.
- Many people opt to reduce their work hours from full-time to part-time in the years before they retire. If you have pursued this option, your income will likely be lower, in turn lowering your tax rate.

- The first years that you draw Social Security benefits can also be years of lower reported income, making it another good time frame in which to convert to a Roth IRA.

One key strategy to handling a Roth IRA conversion is to ***always be able to pay the cost of the tax conversion with outside money***. Structuring your tax year to include something like a significant deduction can help you offset the conversion tax. This way you aren't forced to take the money you need for taxes from the value of the IRA. The reason taxes apply to this maneuver is because when you withdraw money from a traditional IRA, it is treated as taxable income by the IRS. Your financial professional, with the help of the CPAs at their firm, may be able to provide you with options like after-tax money, itemized deductions or other situations that can pose effective tax avoidance options.

Some examples of avoiding Roth IRA conversions taxes include:

- *Using medical expenses that are above 10 percent of your Adjusted Gross Income.* If you have health care costs that you can list as itemized deductions, you can convert an amount of income from a traditional IRA to a Roth IRA that is offset by the deductible amount. Essentially, deductible medical expenses negate the taxes resulting from recording the conversion.
- *Individuals, usually small business owners, who are dealing with a Net Operating Loss (NOL).* If you have NOLs, but aren't able to utilize all of them on your tax return, you can carry them forward to offset the taxable income from the taxes on income you convert to a Roth IRA.
- *Charitable giving.* If you are charitably inclined, you can use the amount of your donations to reduce the amount of taxable income you have during that year. By matching the amount you convert to a Roth IRA to the amount

your taxable income was reduced by charitable giving, you can essentially avoid taxation on the conversion. You may decide to double your donations to a charity in one year, giving them two years' worth of donations in order to offset the Roth IRA conversion tax on this year's tax return.

- *Investments that are subject to depletion.* Certain investments can kick off depletion expenses. If you make an investment and are subject to depletion expenses, they can be deducted and used to offset a Roth IRA conversion tax.

Not all of the above scenarios work for everyone, and there are many other options for offsetting conversion taxes. The point is that you have options, and your financial professional and tax professional can help you understand those options.

If you have a traditional IRA, Roth conversions are something you should look at. As you approach retirement you should consider your options and make choices that keep more of your money in your pocket, not the government's.

## ADDITIONAL TAX BENEFITS OF ROTH IRAS

Not only do Roth IRAs provide you with tax-advantaged growth, they also give you a tax diversified landscape that allows you to maximize your distributions. Chances are that no matter the circumstances, you will have taxed income and other assets subject to taxation. *But if you have a Roth IRA, you have the unique ability to manage your Adjusted Gross Income (AGI), because you have a tax-advantaged income option!*

Converting to a Roth IRA can also help you preserve and build your legacy. Because Roth IRAs are exempt from RMDs, after you make a conversion from a traditional IRA, your Roth account can grow tax-advantaged for another 15, 20 or 25 years and it can be used as tax-advantaged income by your heirs. It is important to note, however, that non-spousal beneficiaries do have to take RMDs from a Roth IRA, or choose to stretch it and draw tax-advantaged income out of it over their lifetime.

## TO CONVERT OR NOT TO CONVERT?

Conversions aren't only for retirees. You can convert at any time. Your choice should be based on your individual circumstances and tax situation. Sticking with a traditional IRA or converting to a Roth, again, depends on your individual circumstances, including your income, your tax bracket and the amount of deductions you have each year.

Is it better to have a Roth IRA or traditional IRA? It depends on your individual circumstance. Some people don't mind having taxable income from an IRA. Their income might not be very high and their RMD might not bump their tax bracket up, so it's not as big a deal. A similar situation might involve income from Social Security. Social Security benefits are taxed based on other income you are drawing. If you are in a position where none or very little of your Social Security benefit is subject to taxes, paying income tax on your RMD may be very easy.

> » *There are also situations where leveraging taxable income from a traditional IRA can work to your advantage come tax time. For example, Ernest and Goudie dream of buying a boat when they retire. It is something they have looked forward to their entire marriage. In addition to the savings and investments that they created to supply them with income during retirement, which includes a traditional IRA, they have also saved money for the sole purpose of purchasing a boat once they stop working.*
>
> *When the time comes and they finally buy the boat of their dreams, they pay an additional $15,000 in sales taxes that year because of the large purchase. Because they are retired*

*and earning less money, the deductions they used to be able to realize from their income taxes are no longer there. The high amount of sales taxes they paid on the boat puts them in a position where they could benefit from taking taxable income from a traditional IRA.*

*When Ernest and Goudie's financial professional learns about their purchase, he immediately contacts a CPA at his firm to run the numbers. They determine that by taking a $15,000 distribution from their IRA, they could fulfill their income needs to offset the $15,000 sales tax deduction that they were claiming due to the purchase of their boat. In the end, they pay zero taxes on their income distribution from their IRA.*

The moral of the story? **Having a tax diversified landscape gives you options.** Having capital assets that can be liquidated, tax-advantaged income options and sources that can create capital gains or capital losses will put you in a position to play your cards right no matter what you want to accomplish with your taxes. The ace up your sleeve is your financial professional and the CPAs they work with. Do yourself a favor and *plan* your taxes instead of *reporting* them!

### CHAPTER 12 QUICK TIP //
- There are many ways to reduce your taxes. Being smart about your Roth IRA conversion is one of the main ways to do so.

# 13
# YOUR LEGACY BEYOND DOLLARS AND CENTS

*"All good men and women must take responsibility to create legacies that will take the next generation to a level we could only imagine."*
*— Jim Rohn*

If you're like most people, planning your estate isn't on the top of your list of things to do. Planning your income needs for retirement, managing your assets and just living your life without worrying about how your estate will be handled when you are gone make legacy planning less than attractive for a Saturday afternoon task. The fact of the matter, however, is that if you don't plan your legacy, someone else will. That someone else is usually a combination of the IRS and other government entities: lawyers, executors, courts, and accountants. Who do you think has the best interests of your beneficiaries in mind?

Today, there is more consideration given to planning a legacy than just maximizing your estate. When most people think about an estate, it may seem like something only the very wealthy have: a stately manor or an enormous business. But a legacy is something else entirely. A legacy is more than the sum of the financial assets you have accumulated. It is the lasting impression you make on those you leave behind. The dollar and cents are just a small part of a legacy.

A legacy encompasses the stories that others tell about you, shared experiences and values. An estate may pay for college tuition, but a legacy may inform your grandchildren about the importance of higher education and self-reliance.

A legacy may also contain family heirlooms or items of emotional significance. It may be a piece of art your great-grandmother painted, family photos, or a childhood keepsake.

When you go about planning your legacy, certainly explore strategies that can maximize the financial benefit to the ones you care about. But also take the time to ensure that you have organized the whole of your legacy, and let that be a part of the last gift you leave.

Many people avoid planning their legacy until they feel they must. Something may change in your life, like the birth of a grandchild, the diagnosis of a serious health problem, or the death of a close friend or loved one. Waiting for tragedy to strike in order to get your affairs in order is not the best course of action. The emotional stress of that kind of situation can make it hard to make patient, thoughtful decisions. Taking the time to create a premeditated and thoughtful legacy plan will assure that your assets will be transferred where and when you want them when the time comes.

## THE BENEFITS OF PLANNING YOUR LEGACY

The distribution of your assets, whether in the form of property, stocks, Individual Retirement Accounts, 401(k)s or liquid assets, can be a complicated undertaking if you haven't left clear instructions about how you want them handled. Not having a plan will cost more money and take more time, leaving your loved ones to wait (sometimes for years) and receive less of your legacy than if you had a clear plan.

Planning your legacy will help your assets be transferred with little delay and little confusion. Instead of leaving decisions about how to distribute your estate to your family, attorneys or financial professionals, preserve your legacy and your wishes by drafting a clear plan at an early age.

And while you know all that, it can still be hard to sit down and do it. It reminds you that life is short, and the relatively complicated nature of sorting through your assets can feel like a daunting task. But one thing is for sure: ***it is impossible for your assets to be transferred or distributed the way you want at the end of your life if you don't have a plan.***

Ask yourself:

- Are my assets up to date?
- Have my primary and contingent beneficiaries been clearly designated?
- Does my plan allow for restriction of a beneficiary?
- Does my legacy plan address minor children that I want to provide with income?
- Does my legacy plan allow for multi-generational payout?

Answers to these questions are critical if you want the final say in how your assets are distributed. In order to achieve your legacy goals, you need a plan.

## MAKING A PLAN

Eventually, when your income need is filled and you have sufficient standby money to meet your need for emergencies, travel or other extra expenses you are planning for, whatever isn't used during your lifetime becomes your financial legacy. The money that you do not use during your lifetime will either go to loved ones, unloved ones, charity, or the IRS. The questions is, who would you rather disinherit?

Another question to ask yourself is, "Do I have a will?" If you haven't taken the time to create one yourself, then you might be surprised to discover that you do have a will: the state you live in has created one for you, and chances are, you won't like how it reads. According to the book "Estate Planning" by Dearborn R&R Newkirk, the "Intestate's" will for Georgia, Section A, states that, "My spouse shall have one-third of my property, and my children will be allowed the other two-thirds, even if they are minor or have no sense of financial responsibility at the time of my death."*

By having a legacy plan that clearly outlines your assets, your beneficiaries and your distribution goals, you can make sure that your money and property is ending up in the hands of the people you determine beforehand. Is it really that big of a deal? It absolutely is. Think about it. Without a clear plan, it is impossible for anyone to know if your beneficiary designations are current and reflect your wishes because you haven't clearly expressed who your beneficiaries are. You may have an idea of who you want your assets to go to, but without a plan, it is anyone's guess. It is also impossible to know if the titling of your assets is accurate unless you have gone through and determined whose name is on the titles. More importantly, *if you have not clearly and effectively*

---

* Estate Planning by Dearborn R&R Newkirk, a division of Dearborn Financial Publishing Inc. copyright 1987, fourth printing 1994.

*communicated your desires regarding the planned distribution of your legacy, you and your family may end up losing a large part of it.*

As you can see, managing a legacy is more complicated than having an attorney read your will, divide your estate and write checks to your heirs. The additional issue of taxes, Family Maximum Benefit calculations and a host of other decisions rear their heads. Educating yourself about the best options for positioning your legacy assets is a challenging undertaking. Working with a financial professional who is versed in determining the most efficient and effective ways of preserving and distributing your legacy can save you time, money and strife.

So, how do you begin?

**Making a Legacy Plan Starts with a Simple List.** The first, and one of the largest, steps to setting up an estate plan with a financial professional that reflects your desires is creating a detailed inventory of your assets and debts (if you have any). You need to know what assets you have, who the beneficiaries are, how much they are worth and how they are titled. You can start by identifying and listing your assets. This is a good starting point for working with a financial professional who can then help you determine the detailed information about your assets that will dictate how they are distributed upon your death.

If you are particularly concerned about leaving your kids and grandkids a lifetime of income with minimal taxes, you will want to discuss a Stretch IRA option with your financial professional.

## STRETCH IRAS: GETTING THE MOST OUT OF YOUR MONEY

In 1986, the U.S. Congress passed a law that allows for multigenerational distributions of IRA assets. This type of distribution is called a Stretch IRA because it stretches the distribution of the account out over a longer period of time to several beneficiaries. It also allows the account to continue accumulating value throughout your relatives' lifetimes. You can use a Stretch IRA as an income tool that distributes throughout your lifetime, your children's lifetimes and your grandchildren's lifetimes.

Stretch IRAs are an attractive option for those more concerned with creating income for their loved ones than leaving them with a lump sum that may be subject to a high tax rate. With traditional IRA distributions, non-spousal beneficiaries must generally take distributions from their inherited IRAs, whether transferred or not, within five years after the death of the IRA owner. An exception to this rule applies if the beneficiary elects to take distributions over his or her lifetime, which is referred to as stretching the IRA.

Let's begin by looking at the potential of stretching an IRA throughout multiple generations.

In this scenario, Mr. Capehart has an IRA with a current balance of $350,000. If we assume a five percent annual rate of return, and a 28 percent tax rate, using the Stretch IRA it can turn a $502,625 legacy into more than $1.5 million. Doubling the value of the IRA also provided Mr. Capehart, his wife, two children and three grandchildren with income. Not choosing the stretch option would have cost nearly $800,000 and had impacts on six of Mr. Capehart's loved ones.

Unfortunately, many things may also play a role in failing to stretch IRA distributions. It can be tempting for a beneficiary to take a lump sum of money despite the tax consequences. Fortunately, if you want to solidify your plan for distribution, there are options that will allow you to open up an IRA and incorporate "spendthrift" clauses for your beneficiaries. This will ensure your legacy is stretched appropriately and to your specifications. Only certain insurance companies allow this option, and you will not find this benefit with any brokerage accounts. You need to work with a financial professional who has the appropriate relationship with an insurance company that provides this option.

## CHAPTER 13 QUICK TIPS //

- Get your estate planning documents in order and create a will. If you don't invest the time to create a will for yourself, your state has one for you, but you might not like how it reads.
- You can take advantage of a "Stretch IRA" to provide income for you, your spouse and your beneficiaries throughout their lifetimes.

# 14
## PREPARING YOUR LEGACY

*"Make a decision or life will make it for you!"*
*–Natasha Nurse*

*Bobby organized his assets long ago. He started planning his retirement early and made investment decisions that would meet his needs. With a combination of IRA to Roth IRA conversions, a series of income annuities and a well-planned money management strategy overseen by his financial professional, he easily filled his income gap and was able to focus on ways to accumulate his wealth throughout his retirement. He reorganized his Know So and Hope So Money as he got older. When Bobby retired, he had an income plan created that allowed him to maximize his Social Security benefit. He even had enough to accumulate wealth during his retirement. At this point, Bobby turned his attention to planning his legacy. He wanted to know how he could maximize the amount of his legacy he will pass on to his heirs.*

*Bobby met with an attorney to draw up a will, but he quickly learned that while having a will was a good plan, it wasn't the most efficient way to distribute his legacy. In fact, relying solely on a will created several roadblocks.*

The two main problems that arose for *Bobby* were *Probate* and *Unintentional Disinheritance:*

## Problem #1: Probate

Probate. Just speaking the word out loud can cause shivers to run down your spine. Probate's ugly reputation is well deserved. It can be a costly, time consuming process that diminishes your estate and can delay the distribution of your estate to your loved ones. Nasty stuff, by any measure. Unless you have made a clear legacy plan and discussed options for avoiding probate, it is highly likely that you have many assets that might pass through probate needlessly. *If your will and beneficiary designations aren't correctly structured, some of these assets will go through the probate process, which can turn dollars into cents.*

If you have a will, probate is usually just a formality. There is little risk that your will won't be executed per your instructions. The problem arises when the costs and lengthy timeline that probate creates come into play. Probate proceedings are notoriously expensive, lengthy and ponderous. A typical probate process identifies all of your assets and debts, pays any taxes and fees that you owe (including estate tax), pays court fees, and distributes your property and assets to your inheritors. This process usually takes at least a year, and can take even longer before your inheritors actually receive anything that you have left for them. For this reason, and because of the sometimes exorbitant fees that may be charged by lawyers and accountants during the process, probate has earned a nasty reputation.

Probate can also be a painstakingly public process. Because the probate process happens in court, the assets you own that go through a probate procedure become part of the public record. While this may not seem like a big deal to some, other people don't want that kind of intimate information available to the public.

Additionally, if your estate is entirely distributed via your will, the money that your family may need to cover the costs of your medical bills, funeral expenses and estate taxes will be tied up in probate, which can last up to a year or more. While immediate family members may have the option of requesting immediate cash from your assets during probate to cover immediate health care expenses, taxes, and fees, that process comes with its own set of complications. Choosing alternative methods for distributing your legacy can make life easier for your loved ones and can help them claim more of your estate in a more timely fashion than traditional methods.

*A simpler and less tedious approach is to avoid probate altogether by structuring your estate to be distributed outside of the probate process.* Two common ways of doing this are by structuring your assets inside a life insurance plan, and by using individual retirement planning tools like IRAs that give you the option of designating a beneficiary upon your death.

## Problem #2: Unintentionally Disinheriting Your Family

You would never want to unintentionally disinherit a loved one or loved ones because of confusion surrounding your legacy plan. Unfortunately, it happens. Why? This terrible situation is typically caused by a simple lack of understanding. In particular, mistakes regarding legacy distribution occur with regards to those whom people care for the most: their grandchildren.

One of the most important ways to plan for the inheritance of your grandchildren is by properly structuring the distribution of your legacy. Specifically, you need to know if your legacy is going to be distributed *per stirpes* or *per capita*.

**Per Stirpes.** *Per stirpes* is a legal term in Latin that means "by the branch." Your estate will be distributed *per stirpes* if you designate each branch of your family to receive an equal share of your estate. In the event that your children predecease you, their share will be distributed evenly between their children—your grandchildren.

**Per Capita.** *Per capita* distribution is different in that you may designate different amounts of your estate to be distributed to members of the same generation.

Per stirpes distribution of assets will follow the family tree down the line as the predecessor beneficiaries pass away. On the other hand, per capita distribution of assets ends on the branch of the family tree with the death of a designated beneficiary. For example, when your child passes away, in a per capita distribution, your grandchildren would not receive distributions from the assets that you designated to your child.

What the terms mean is not nearly as important as what they do, however. The reality is that improperly titled assets could accidentally leave your grandchildren disinherited upon the death of their parents. It's easy to check, and it's even easier to fix.

A simple way to remember the difference between the two types of distribution goes something like this: "***Stirpes are forever and Capita is capped.***"

Another way to avoid complicated legacy distribution problems, and the probate process, is by leveraging a life insurance plan.

## LIFE INSURANCE: AN IMPORTANT LEGACY TOOL

One of the most powerful legacy tools you can leverage is a good life insurance policy. Life insurance is a highly efficient legacy tool because it creates money when it is needed or desired the most. Over the years, life insurance has become less expensive, while it offers more features, and it provides longer guarantees.

There are many unique benefits of life insurance that can help your beneficiaries get the most out of your legacy. Some of them include:

- Providing beneficiaries with a tax-free, liquid asset.
- Covering the costs associated with your death.
- Providing income for your dependents.
- Offering an investment opportunity for your beneficiaries.
- Covering expenses such as tuition or mortgage down payments for your children or grandchildren.

Very few people want life insurance, but nearly everyone wants what it does. Life insurance is specifically, and uniquely, capable of creating money when it is needed most. When a loved one passes, no amount of money can remove the pain of loss. And certainly, money doesn't solve the challenges that might arise with losing someone important.

It has been said that when you have money, you have options. When you don't have money, your options are severely limited. You might imagine a life insurance policy can give your family and loved ones options that would otherwise be impossible.

> » *Jeff spent the last 20 years building a small business. In so many ways, it is a family business. Each of his three children, Maddie, Ruby and Edward, worked in the shop part-time during high school. But after all three attended college, only Maddie returned to join her father, and eventually will run the business full-time when Ben retires.*
>
> *Jeff is able to retire comfortably on Social Security and on-going income from the shop, but the business is nearly his entire financial legacy. It is his wish that Maddie own the business outright, but he also wants to leave an equal legacy to each of his three children.*

*There is no simple way to divide the business into thirds and still leave the business intact for Maddie.*

*Jeff ends up buying a life insurance policy to make up the difference. Ruby and Edward will receive their share of an inheritance in cash from the life insurance policy and Maddie will be able to inherit the business intact.*

*Jeff is able to accomplish his goals, treat all three children equitably and leave Maddie the business she helped to build.*

If you have a life insurance policy but you haven't looked at it in a while, you may not know how it operates, how much it is worth and how it will be distributed to your beneficiaries. You may also need to update your beneficiaries on your policy. In short, without a comprehensive review of your policy, you don't really know where the money will go or to whom it will go.

If you don't have a life insurance policy but are looking for options to maintain and grow your legacy, speaking with a professional can show you the benefits of life insurance. Many people don't consider buying a life insurance policy until some event in their life triggers it, like the loss of a loved one, an accident or a health condition.

## BENEFITS OF LIFE INSURANCE

Life insurance is a useful and secure tool for contingency planning, ensuring that your dependents receive the assets that you want them to have, and for meeting the financial goals you have set for the future. While it bears the name "Life Insurance," it is, in reality, a diverse financial tool that can meet many needs. The main function of a life insurance policy is to provide financial assets for your survivors. Life insurance is particularly efficient at achieving this goal because it provides a tax-advantaged lump sum of money in the form of a death benefit to your beneficiary or beneficiaries. That financial asset can be used in a number of ways. It can be structured as an investment to provide income for your spouse or children, it can pay down debts, and it can be used to cover estate taxes and other costs associated with death.

Tax liabilities on the estate you leave behind are inevitable. Capital property, for instance, is taxed at its fair market value at the time of your death, unless that property is transferred to your spouse. If the property has appreciated during the time you owned it, taxation on capital gains will occur. Registered Retirement Savings Plans (RRSPs) and other similarly structured assets are also included as taxable income unless transferred to a beneficiary as well. Those are just a few examples of how an estate can become subject to a heavy tax burden. The unique benefits of a life insurance policy provide ways to handle this tax burden, solving any liquidity problems that may arise if your family members want to hold onto an illiquid asset, such as a piece of property or an investment. Life insurance can provide a significant amount of money to a family member or other beneficiary, and that money is likely to remain exempt from taxation or seizure.

One of life insurance's most important benefits is that it is not considered part of the estate of the policy holder. The death benefit that is paid by the insurance company goes exclusively to the beneficiaries listed on the policy. This shields the proceeds of the policy from fees and costs that can reduce an estate, including probate proceedings, attorneys' fees and claims made by creditors. The distribution of your life insurance policy is also unaffected by delays of the estate's distribution, like probate. Your beneficiaries will get the proceeds of the policy in a timely fashion, regardless of how long it takes for the rest of your estate to be settled.

Investing a portion of your assets in a life insurance policy can also protect that portion of your estate from creditors. If you owe money to someone or some entity at the time of your death, a creditor is not able to claim any money from a life insurance policy or an annuity, for that matter. An exception to this rule is if you had already used the life insurance policy as collateral against a loan. If a large portion of the money you want to dedicate to your legacy is sitting in a savings account, investment or other liquid form, creditors may be able to receive their claim on it before your beneficiaries get anything that is if there's anything left. A life insurance policy protects your assets from creditors and ensures that your beneficiaries get the money that you intend them to have.

## HOW MUCH LIFE INSURANCE DO YOU NEED?

Determining the type of policy and the amount right for you depends on an analysis of your needs. A financial professional can help you complete a needs analysis that will highlight the amount of insurance that you require to meet your goals. This type of personalized review will allow you to determine ways to continue providing income for your spouse or any dependents you may have. A financial professional can also help you calculate the amount of income that your policy should replace to meet the needs of your beneficiaries and the duration of the distribution of that income.

You may also want to use your life insurance policy to meet any expenses associated with your death. These can include funeral costs, fees from probate and legal proceedings, and taxes. You may also want to dedicate a portion of your policy proceeds to help fund tuition or other expenses for your children or grandchildren. You can buy a policy and hope it covers all of those costs, or you can work with a professional who can calculate exactly how much insurance you need and how to structure it to meet your goals. Which would you rather do?

## AVOIDING POTENTIAL SNAGS

There are benefits to having life insurance supersede the direction given in a will or other estate plan, but there are also some potential snags that you should address to meet your wishes. For example, if your will instructs that your assets be divided equally between your two children but your life insurance beneficiary is listed as just one of the children, the assets in the life insurance policy will only be distributed to the child listed as the beneficiary. The beneficiary designation of your life insurance supersedes your will's instruction. This is important to understand when designating beneficiaries on a policy you purchase. Work with a professional to make sure that your beneficiaries are accurately listed on your assets, especially your life insurance policies.

## USING LIFE INSURANCE TO BUILD YOUR LEGACY

Depending on your goals, there are strategies you can use that could multiply how much you leave behind. Life insurance is one of the most surefire and efficient investment tools for building a substantial legacy that will meet your financial goals.

Here is a brief overview of how life insurance can boost your legacy:

- Life insurance provides an immediate increase in your legacy.
- It provides an income tax-advantaged death benefit for your beneficiaries.
- A good life insurance policy has the opportunity to accumulate value over time.
- It may have an option to include long-term care (LTC) or chronic illness benefits should you require them.

If your Green Money income needs for retirement are met and you have Yellow Money assets that will provide for your future expenses, you may have extra assets that you want to earmark as legacy funds. By electing to invest those assets into a life insurance policy, you can immediately increase the amount of your legacy. Remember, **life insurance allows you to transfer**

**a tax-advantaged lump sum of money to your beneficiaries. It remains in your control during your lifetime, can provide for your long-term care needs and bypasses probate costs.** And make no mistake, taxes can have a huge impact on your legacy. Not only that, income and assets from your legacy can have tax implications for your beneficiaries, as well.

Here's a brief overview of how taxes could affect your legacy and your beneficiaries:

- The higher your income, the higher the rate at which it is taxed.
- Withdrawals from qualified plans are taxed as income.
- What's more, when you leave a large qualified plan, it ends up being taxed at a high rate.
- If you left a $500,000 IRA to your child, they could end up owing as much as $140,000 in income taxes.
- However, if you could just withdraw $50,000 a year, the tax bill might only be $10,000 per year.

How could you use that annual amount to leave a larger legacy? Luckily, you can leverage a life insurance policy to avoid those tax penalties, preserving a larger amount of your legacy and freeing your beneficiaries from an added tax burden.

> » *When Chris turned 70 years old, she decided it was time to look into life insurance policy options. She still feels young, but she remembers that her mother died in early 70s, and she wants to plan ahead so she can pass on some of her legacy to her grandchildren just like her grandmother did for her.*
>
> *Chris doesn't really want to think about life insurance, but she does want the security, reliability and tax-advantaged distribution that it offers. She lives modestly, and her Social Security benefit meets most of her income needs. As the beneficiary of her late husband's Certificate of Deposit (CD), she*

*has $100,000 in an account that she has never used and doesn't anticipate ever needing since her income needs were already met.*

*After looking at several different investment options with a professional, Chris decides that a Single Premium life insurance policy fits her needs best. She can buy the policy with a $100,000 one-time payment and she is guaranteed that it would provide more than the value of the contract to her beneficiaries. If she left the money in the CD, it would be subject to taxes. But for every dollar that she puts into the life insurance policy, her beneficiaries are guaranteed at least that dollar plus a death benefit, and all of it will be **tax-free!***

*For $100,000, Chris's particular policy offers a $170,000 death benefit distribution to her beneficiaries. By moving the $100,000 from a CD to a life insurance policy, Chris increases her legacy by 70 percent. Not only that, she has also sheltered it from taxes, so her beneficiaries will be able to receive $1.70 for every $1.00 that she entered into the policy! While buying the policy doesn't allow her to use the money for herself, it does allow her family to benefit from her well-planned legacy.*

## MAKE YOUR WISHES KNOWN

Estate taxes used to be a much hotter topic in the mid-2000s when the estate tax limits and exclusions were much smaller and taxed at a higher rate than today. In 2008, estates valued at $2 million or more were taxed at 45 percent. Just two years later, the limit was raised to $5 million dollars taxed at 35 percent. The limit has continued to rise ever since. The limit applies to fewer people than before. Estate organization, however, is just as important as ever, and it affects everyone.

Ask yourself:

- Are your assets actually titled and held the way you think they are?
- Are your beneficiaries set up the way you think they should be?
- Have there been changes to your family or those you desire as beneficiaries?

There is more to your legacy beyond your property, money, investments and other assets that you leave to family members, loved ones and charities. Everyone has a legacy beyond money. You also leave behind personal items of importance, your values and beliefs, your personal and family history, and your wishes. Beyond a will and a plan for your assets, it is important that you make your wishes known to someone for the rest of your personal legacy. When it comes time for your family and loved ones to make decisions after you are gone, knowing your wishes can help them make decisions that honor you and your legacy, and give meaning to what you leave behind. Your professional can help you organize.

Think about your:
- Personal stories / recollections
- Values
- Personal items of emotional significance
- Financial assets

Do you want to make a plan to pass these things on to your family?

## WORKING WITH A PROFESSIONAL
Part of using life insurance to your greatest advantage is selecting the policy and provider that can best meet your goals. Venturing into the jungle of policies, brokers and salespeople can be overwhelming, and can leave you wondering if you've made the best decision. Working with a trusted financial professional can help

you cut through the red tape, the "sales-speak" and confusion to find a policy that meets your goals and best serves your desires for your money. If you already have a policy, a financial professional can help you review it and become familiar with the policy's premium, the guarantees the policy affords, its performance, and its features and benefits. A financial professional can also help you make any necessary changes to the policy.

> *When Becky turned 88, her daughter finally convinced her to meet with a financial professional to help her organize her assets and get her legacy in order. Although Becky is reluctant to let a stranger in on her personal finances, she ends up very glad that she did.*
>
> *In the process of listing Becky's assets and her beneficiaries, her professional finds a man's name listed as the beneficiary of an old life insurance annuity that she owns. It turns out, the man is Becky's ex-husband who is still alive. Had Becky passed away before her ex-husband, the annuities and any death benefits that came with them, would have been passed on to her ex-husband. This does not reflect her latest wishes.*

Things change, relationships evolve and the way you would like your legacy organized needs to adapt to the changes that happen throughout your life. There may be a new child or grandchild in your family, or you may have been divorced or remarried. A professional will regularly review your legacy assets and ask you questions to make sure that everything is up to date and that the current organization reflects your current wishes.

## CHAPTER 14 QUICK TIPS //

- Your legacy encompasses more than just the physical assets left behind for your children. It encompasses the ideals and values important to you.
- Life insurance provides for the distribution of tax-free, liquid assets to your beneficiaries and can significantly build your legacy.

# 15

# CHOOSING A FINANCIAL PROFESSIONAL

From the moment you set out on the road of your retirement journey to the point where you start seeing the sites, your assets organized, your income needs met, and your accumulation and legacy plans in place, working with a professional that you trust can make all the difference in how smoothly things go along the way.

It is important to know what you are looking for before you head too far down the wrong road. There are many people that would love to handle your money, but not everyone is qualified to handle it in a way that leads to a holistic approach to creating a solid retirement plan.

The distinction being made here is that you should look for someone that puts your interests first and actively wants to help you meet your goals and objectives. Oftentimes, the products someone sells you matter less than their dedication to making sure that you have a plan that meets your needs.

Professionals take your whole financial position into consideration. They make plans that adjust your risk exposure, invest in tools that secure your desired income during retirement and create investment strategies that allow you to continue accumulating wealth during your retirement for you to use later or to contribute to your legacy. If you buy stocks with a broker, use a different agent for a life insurance policy and have an unmanaged 401(k) through your employer, working with a financial professional will consolidate the management of your assets so you have one trustworthy person quarterbacking all of the team elements of your portfolio. Financial products and investment tools change, but the concepts that lie behind wise retirement planning are lasting. In the end, a financial professional's approach is designed for those serious about planning for retirement. *Can you say the same thing about the person that advises you about your financial life?*

It's easy to see how choosing a financial professional can be one of the most important decisions you can make in your life. Not only do they provide you with advice, they also manage the personal assets that supply your retirement income and contribute to your legacy. So, how do you find a good one?

## HOW TO FIND A FINANCIAL PROFESSIONAL YOU CAN TRUST

Taking care to select a financial professional is one of the best things you can do for yourself and for your future. Your professional has influence and control of your investment decisions, making their role in your life more than just important. Your financial security and the quality of your retirement depends on the decisions, investment strategies and asset structuring that you and your professional create.

Working with a professional is different than calling up a broker when you want to buy or trade some stock. This isn't a decision that you can hand off to anyone else. You need to bring your time and attention to the table when it comes to finding someone with whom you can entrust your financial life. Separating the wheat from the chaff will take some work, but you'll be happy you did it.

While no one can tell you exactly who to choose or how to choose them, the following information can help you narrow the field:

## NARROWING THE FIELD

**1. Decide on the Type of Professional with Whom You Want to Work.** There are four basic kinds of financial professionals. Many professionals may play overlapping roles. It is important to know a professional's primary function, how they charge for their services and whether they are obligated to act in your best interest.

*Registered representatives*, better known as stockbrokers or bank / investment representatives, make their living by earning commissions on insurance products and investment services. Stockbrokers basically sell you things. The products from which they make the highest commission are sometimes the products that they recommend to their clients. If you want to make a simple transaction, such as buying or selling a particular stock, a registered representative can help you. Although registered representatives are licensed professionals, if you want to create a structured and integrated approach to positioning your assets for retirement, you might want to consider continuing your search.

The term "planner" is often misused. It can refer to credible professionals that are CPAs, CFPs and ChFCs to your uncle's next door neighbor who claims to have a lead on some undervalued stock about to be "discovered." A wide array of people may claim to be planners because there are no requirements to be a planner. The term financial planner, however, refers to someone who is properly registered as an investment advisor and serves as a fiduciary as described below.

Financial professionals are the diamonds in the rough. These Registered Investment Advisors are compensated on a fee basis. They do, however, often have licensure as stockbrokers or insurance agents, allowing them to earn commissions on certain transactions. More importantly, **financial professionals are financial fiduciaries, meaning they are required to make financial decisions in your best interest and reflecting your risk tolerance.** Investment Advisors are held to high ethical standards and are highly regarded in the financial industry. Financial professionals also often take a more comprehensive approach to asset management. These professionals are trained and credentialed to plan and coordinate their clients' assets in order to meet their goals or retirement and legacy planning. They are not focused on individual stocks, investments or markets. They look at the big picture, the whole enchilada.

*Money managers are* on par with financial professionals. However, they are often given explicit permission to make investment decisions without advanced approval by their clients.

Understanding who you are working with and what their title is the first step to planning your retirement. While each of the above-mentioned types of financial professionals can help you with aspects of your finances, it is **financial professionals** who have the most intimate role, the most objective investment strategies and the most unbiased mode of compensation for their services. A financial professional can also help you with the non-financial aspects of your legacy and can help you find ways to create a tax planning strategy to help you save money.

**2. Be Objective.** At the end of the day, you need to separate the weak from the strong. While you might want a strong personal rapport with your professional, or you may want to choose your professional for their personality and positive attitude, it is more important that you find someone who will give wise advice regarding achieving your retirement goals.

Make sure they represent a firm that has the investment tools and products that you desire, and make sure they have experience in retirement planning. That is, after all, the main goal.

Don't be afraid to investigate each of your candidates. You'll want to ask the same questions and look for the same information from everyone you consider so you can then compare them and discern which is best for you. You'll want to take a look at the specific credentials of each professional, their experience and competence, their ethics and fiduciary status, their history and track record, and a list of the services that they offer. The professionals who meet all or most of your qualifications are the ones you will contact for an interview.

Potential professionals should meet your qualifications in the following categories:

- *Credentials:* Look at their experience, the quality of their education, any associations to which they belong and certifications they have earned. Someone who has continued their professional education through ongoing certifications will be more up-to-date on current financial practices compared to someone who got their degree 25 years ago and hasn't done a thing since.
- *Practices:* Look at the track record of your candidates, how they are compensated for their services, the reports and analysis they offer, and their value added services.
- *Services:* Your professional must meet your needs. If you are planning your retirement, you should work with someone who offers services that help you to that end. You want someone who can offer planning, advice on investment strategies, ways to calculate risk, advice on insurance and annuities products, and ways to manage your tax strategy.

- *Ethics:* You want to work with someone who is above board and does things the right way. Vet them by checking their compliance record, current licensing, fiduciary status and, yes, even their criminal record. You never know!

**3. Ask for and Check References.** Every professional should be able to provide you with at least two or three names. In fact, they will probably be eager to share them with you. Most professionals rely on references for validation of their success, quality of services and likability. You should, however, take them with a grain of salt. You have no way to know whether or not references are a professional's friends or colleagues.

It is worth contacting references, however, to check for inconsistencies. Ask each reference the same set of questions to get the same basic information. How long have they been working with the professional? What kind of services have they used and were they happy with them? What type of financial planning did they use the professional for? Were they versed in the type of financial planning that you needed? Questions like these can help you get a sense of how well the reference knows their professional and whether or not they are a quality reference.

A good reference is a bit like icing on the cake. It's nice to have them, but nothing speaks louder than a good track record and quality experience. And remember that a good reference, while nice to hear, is relatively cheap. How many times have you heard someone on the golf course or at work telling you how great their stockbroker is? But how many times have you heard about the bad investments or losses they have experienced?

## HOW TO INTERVIEW CANDIDATES

After vetting your candidates and narrowing down a list of professionals that you think might be a good fit for you, it's time to start interviewing.

When you meet in person with a professional, you want to take advantage of your time with them. The presentations and information that they share with you will be important to pay attention to, but you will also want to control some aspects of the interview. After a professional has told you what they want you to hear, it's time to ask your own questions to get the specific information you need to make your decision.

Make sure to prepare a list of questions and an informal agenda so that you can keep track of what you want to ask and what points you want the professional to touch on during the interview. Using the same questions and agenda will also allow you to more easily compare the professionals after you have interviewed them all. Remember that these interviews are just that, *interviews*. You are meeting with several professionals to determine with whom you want to work. Don't agree to anything or sign anything during an interview until after you have made your final decision.

It can also be helpful to put a time limit on your interviews and to meet the professionals at their offices. The time limit will keep things on track and will allow structured time for presentations and questions/discussion. By meeting them at their office, you can get a sense of the work environment, the staff culture and attitude, and how the firm does business. If you are unable to travel to a professional's office and must meet them at your home or office, make sure that your interviews are scheduled with plenty of time between so the professionals don't cross each other's paths.

You can use the following questions during an initial interview to get an understanding of how each professional does business and whether they are a good fit for you:

**1. How do you charge for your services? How much do you charge?** This information should be easy to find on their website, but if you don't see it, ask. Find out if they charge an initial planning fee, if they charge a percentage for assets under their management and if they make money by selling specific financial products or services. If so, you should follow up by asking how much the service costs. This will give you an idea of how they really make their money and if they have incentive to sell certain products over others. Make sure you understand exactly how you will be charged so there are no surprises down the road if you decide to work with this person.

**2. What are your credentials, licenses, and certifications?** There are Certified Financial Planners (CFPs), Chartered Financial Consultants (ChFCs), Investment Advisor Representatives, Certified Public Accountants (CPAs) and Personal Financial Specialists (PFSs). Whatever their credentials or titles, you want to be sure that the professional you work with is an expert in the field relevant to your circumstances. If you want someone to manage your money, you will most likely look for an Investment Advisor. Someone that works with an independent firm will likely have a team of CPAs, CFPs and other financial experts upon whom they can draw. If you like the professional you are meeting with and you think they might be a good fit, but they don't have the accounting experience you want them to have, ask about their firm and the resources available to them. If they work closely with CPAs that are experienced in your needs, it could be a good match.

**3. What are the financial services that you and your firm provide?** The question within the question here is, "Can you help me achieve my goals?" Some people can only provide you with investment advice, and others are tax consultants. You will likely want to work with someone that provides a complete suite of financial planning services and products that touch on retirement planning, insurance options, legacy and estate structuring, and tax planning. Whatever services they provide, make sure they meet your needs and your anticipated needs.

**4. What kinds of clients do you work with the most?** A lot of financial professionals work within a niche: retirement planning, risk assessment, life insurance, etc. Finding someone who works with other people that are in the same financial boat as you and who have similar goals can be an important way to make sure they understand your needs. While someone might be a crackerjack annuities cowboy, you might not be interested in that option. Ask follow-up questions that will really help you understand where their expertise lies and whether or not their experience lines up with your needs.

**5. How do you approach investing?** You may be entirely in the dark about how to approach your investments, or you might have some guiding principles. Either way, ask each candidate what their philosophy is. Some will resonate with you and some won't. A good professional who has a realistic approach to investing won't promise you the moon or tell you that they can make you a lot of money. Professionals who are successful at retirement planning and full service financial management will tell you that they will listen to your goals, risk tolerance and comfort level with different types of investment strategies. Working with someone that you trust is critical, and this question in particular can help you find out who you can and who you can't.

**6. How do you remain in contact with your clients?** Does your prospective professional hold annual, quarterly or monthly meetings? How often do *you* want to meet with your professional? Some people want to check in once a year, go over everything and make sure their ducks are all in a row. If any changes over the previous year or additions to their legacy planning strategy came up, they'll do it on that date. Other people want a monthly update to be more involved in the decision making process and to understand what's happening with their portfolio. You basically need to determine the right degree of involvement for both you and your financial professional. You'll also want to feel out how your professional communicates. Do you prefer phone calls or face-to-face meetings? Do you want your professional to explain things to you in detail or to summarize for you what decisions they've made? Is the professional willing to give you their direct phone number or their email address? More importantly, do you want that information and do you want to be able to contact them in those ways?

**8. Did they ask questions and show signs that they were interested in working with me?** A professional who will structure your assets to reflect your risk tolerance and to position you for a comfortable retirement must be a good listener. You will want to pass by a professional who talks non-stop and tells you what to do without listening to what you want them to do. If you felt they listened well and understood your needs, and seemed interested and experienced in your situation, then they might be right for you.

## THE IMPORTANCE OF INDEPENDENCE

Not all investment firms and financial professionals are created equal. The information in this book has systematically shown that leveraging investments for income and accumulation in today's market requires new ideas and modern planning. In short, you need innovative ideas to come up with the creative solutions that will provide you with the retirement that you want. Innovation thrives on independence. No matter how good a financial professional is, the firm that they represent needs to operate on principles that make sense in today's economy. Remember, advice about money has been around forever. Good advice, however, changes with the times.

Timing the market, relying on the sale of stocks for income and banking on high treasury and bond returns are not strategies. They aren't even realistic ways to make money or to generate income. Working with an independent agent can help you break free from the old ways of thinking and position you to create a realistic retirement plan.

Working with an independent professional who relies on fee-based income tied to the success of their performance will also give you greater peace of mind. When you do well, they do well, and that's the way it should be. Your independent financial professional will make sure that:

- Your assets are organized and structured to reflect your risk tolerance.
- Your assets will be available to you when you need them and in the way that you need them.
- You will have a lifetime income that will support your lifestyle through your retirement.
- You are handling your taxes as efficiently as possible.
- Your legacy is in order.
- Your Red Money is turned into Yellow Money, and is managed in your best interest.

*» Remember Steve and Carol from Chapter 2? Even though they knew they had Social Security benefits coming, they placed some money in savings and each had a pension or a 401(k). Before they met with a financial professional, they had no idea what their retirement would look like. After they met with an agent, they knew exactly what types of assets they had, how much they were worth, how much risk they were exposed to and how they were going to be distributed. They also created an income plan so that they could pay their bills every month the moment they retired, and they maximized their Social Security benefit by targeting the year and month they*

*would get the most lifetime benefits. After their income needs were met, they were able to continue accumulating wealth by investing their extra assets to serve them in the future and contribute to their legacy. Their professional also helped them make decisions that impacted their taxes, protecting the value of their assets and allowing them to keep more of their money.*

*This isn't a fairy tale scenario. This is an example of how much you stand to gain by meeting with a financial professional who can help you create a thoughtful approach to your retirement. The concept of Know So and Hope So didn't just apply to their money, it also applied to Steve and Carol. They hoped that they would have enough for retirement and that they had worked hard enough and saved enough to maintain their lifestyle. Working with a financial professional allowed them to know that their income needs were secured and structured to provide them with income for the rest of their lives and with some money to spare.*

*Now, ask yourself: Is your retirement built on hopes and dreams, or a solid, predictable plan?*

Finding, interviewing and selecting a financial professional can seem like a daunting task. And honestly, it will take a good amount of work to narrow the field and find the one you want. In the end, it is worth the blood, sweat and tears. Your retirement, lifestyle, assets and legacy is on the line. The choices you make today will have lasting impacts on your life and the life of your loved ones. Working with someone you trust and know you can rely on to make decisions that will benefit you is invaluable. The work it takes to find them is something you will never regret.

I've heard it said that the quality of our lives is determined by the quality of our relationships. Commit to building or rebuilding strong relationships, not just professionally, but with friends and family. Commit to having a strong and healthy body—take care of it—because it's the only place you really have to live in on this earth.

When it's all said and done, those who have the strongest retirements are the people who commit to having something to retire TO versus from. Staying strong financially, physically, and relationally with friends, family, and God will all lead to mental, emotional, and spiritual strength, and this, ultimately, will give you the best chance at having the fun and fulfilling retirement you have always dreamed of achieving.

## CHAPTER 15 QUICK TIPS //

- When choosing a financial professional to help you navigate the retirement journey, make sure you look for a fiduciary professional who is legally required to make decisions that are in your best interest at all times.

- If you feel you have more *Hope So* than *Know So* about your money and what your retirement is going to look like, working with a financial professional will give you clarity and confidence about what decisions are best for you.

- It is difficult for investors to not make emotional decisions about their investments. Financial professionals work with your risk tolerance, income needs and assets to find the most logical, efficient and beneficial way for you to structure your investments.

- Not all investment firms and financial professionals are created equal. Working with an independent professional will give you more options that are customized to your life.

- If you'd like to schedule a complementary consultation to see if your retirement is on track, don't hesitate to call me, Eric T. Scoggins, CFP, at 770-652-3496.

# GLOSSARY*

**ANNUAL RESET** *(ANNUAL RATCHET, CLIQUET)* – Crediting methods measuring index movement over a one year period. Positive interest is calculated and credited at the end of each contract year and cannot be lost if the index subsequently declines. Say that the index increased from 100 to 110 in one year and the indexed annuity had an 80 percent participation rate. The insurance company would take the 10 percent gross index gain for the year (110-100/100), apply the participation rate (10 percent index gain x 80 percent rate) and credit 8 percent interest to the annuity. But, what if in the following year the index declined back to 100? The individual would keep the 8 percent interest earned and simply receive zero interest for the down year. An annual reset structure

---

* *"Glossary of Terms." FixedAnnuityFacts.com. NAFA, the National Association for Fixed Annuities, n.d. 12 Nov. 2013*

preserves credited gains and treats negative index periods as years with zero growth.

**ANNUITANT** – The person, usually the annuity owner, whose life expectancy is used to calculate the income payment amount on the annuity.

**ANNUITY** – An annuity is a contract issued by an insurance company that often serves as a type of savings plan used by individuals looking for long term growth and protection of assets that will likely be needed within retirement.

**AVERAGING** – Index values may either be measured from a start point to an end point (point-to-point) or values between the start point and end point may be averaged to determine an ending value. Index values may be averaged over the days, weeks, months or quarters of the period.

**BENEFICIARY** – A beneficiary is the person designated to receive payments due upon the death of the annuity owner or the annuitant themselves.

**BONUS RATE** – A bonus rate is the "extra" or "additional" interest paid during the first year (the initial guarantee period), typically used as an added incentive to get consumers to select their annuity policy over another.

**CALL OPTION** *(ALSO SEE PUT OPTION)* – Gives the holder the right to buy an underlying security or index at a specified price on or before a given date.

**CAP** – The maximum interest rate that will be credited to the annuity for the year or period. The cap usually refers to the maximum interest credited after applying the participation rate or yield spread. If the index methodology showed a 20 percent increase, the participation rate was 60 percent and the maximum interest cap was 10 percent, the contract would credit 10 percent interest. A few annuities use a maximum gain cap instead of a maximum interest cap with the participation rate or yield spread applied to the lesser of the gain or the cap. If the index methodology showed a 20 percent increase, the participation rate was 60 percent and the maximum gain cap was 10 percent, the contract would credit 6 percent interest.

**COMPOUND INTEREST** – Interest is earned on both the original principal and on previously earned interest. It is more favorable than simple interest. Suppose that your original principal was $1 and your interest rate was 10 percent for five years. With simple interest, your value is ($1 + $0.10 interest each year) = $1.50. With compound interest, your value is ($1 x 1.10 x 1.10 x 1.10 x 1.10 x 1.10) = $1.61. The advantage of compound interest over simple interest becomes greater as each subsequent period passes.

**CREDITING METHOD** *(ALSO SEE <u>METHODOLOGY</u>)* – The formula(s) used to determine the excess interest that is credited above the minimum interest guarantee.

**DEATH BENEFITS** – The payment the annuity owner's estate or beneficiaries will receive if he or she dies before the annuity matures. On most annuities, this is equal to the current account value. Some annuities offer an enhanced value at death via an optional rider that has a monthly or annual fee associated with it.

**EXCESS INTEREST** – Interest credited to the annuity contract above the minimum guaranteed interest rate. In an indexed annuity the excess interest is determined by applying a stated crediting method to a specific index or indices.

**FIXED ANNUITY** – A contract issued by an insurance company guaranteeing a minimum interest rate with the crediting of excess interest determined by the performance of the insurer's general account. Index annuities are fixed annuities.

**FIXED DEFERRED ANNUITY** – With fixed annuities, an insurance company offers a guaranteed interest rate plus safety of your principal and earnings ((subject to the claims-paying ability of the insurance company). Your interest rate will be reset periodically, based on economic and other factors, but is guaranteed to never fall below a certain rate.

**FREE WITHDRAWALS** – Withdrawals that are free of surrender charges.

**INDEX** – The underlying external benchmark upon which the crediting of excess interest is based, also a measure of the prices of a group of securities.

**IRA** *(INDIVIDUAL RETIREMENT ACCOUNT)* – An IRA is a tax-advantaged personal savings plan that lets an individual set aside money for retirement. All or part of the participant's contributions may be tax deductible, depending on the type of IRA chosen and the participant's personal financial circumstances. Distributions from many employer-sponsored retirement plans may be eligible to be rolled into an IRA to continue tax-deferred growth until the funds are needed. An annuity can be used as an IRA; that is, IRA funds can be used to purchase an annuity.

**IRA ROLLOVER** – IRA rollover is the phrase used when an individual who has a balance in an employer-sponsored retirement plan transfers that balance into an IRA. Such an exchange, when properly handled, is a tax-advantaged transaction.

**LIQUIDITY** – The ease with which an asset is convertible to cash. An asset with high liquidity provides flexibility, in that the owner can easily convert it to cash at any time, but it also tends to decrease profitability.

**MARKET RISK** – The risk of the market value of an asset fluctuating up or down over time. In a fixed or fixed indexed annuity, the original principal and credited interest are not subject to market risk. Even if the index declines, the annuity owner would receive no less than their original principal back if they decided to cash in the policy at the end of the surrender period. Unlike a security, indexed annuities guarantee the original premium and the premium is backed by, and is as safe as, the insurance company that issued it (subject to the claims-paying ability of the insurance company).

**METHODOLOGY** *(ALSO SEE CREDITING METHOD)* – The way that interest crediting is calculated. On fixed indexed annuities, there are a variety of different methods used to determine how index movement becomes interest credited.

**MINIMUM GUARANTEED RETURN** *(MINIMUM INTEREST RATE)* – Fixed indexed annuities typically provide a minimum guaranteed return over the life of the contract. At the time that the owner chooses to terminate the contract, the cash surrender value is compared to a second value calculated using the minimum guaranteed return and the higher of the two values is paid to the annuity owner.

**OPTION** – A contract which conveys to its holder the right, but not the obligation, to buy or sell something at a specified price on or before a given date. After this given date the option ceases to exist. Insurers typically buy options to provide for the excess interest potential. Options may be American style whereby they may be exercised at any time prior to the given date, or they may have to be exercised only during a specified window. Options that may only be exercised during a specified period are European-style options.

**OPTION RISK** – Most insurers create the potential for excess interest in an indexed annuity by buying options. Say that you could buy a share of stock for $50. If you bought the stock and it rose to $60 you could sell it and net a $10 profit. But, if the stock price fell to $40 you'd have a $10 loss. Instead of buying the actual stock, we could buy an option that gave us the right to buy the stock for $50 at any time over the next year. The cost of the option is $2. If the stock price rose to $60 we would exercise our option, buy the stock at $50 and make $10 (less the $2 cost of the option). If the price of the stock fell to $40, $30 or $10, we wouldn't use the option and it would expire. The loss is limited to $2—the cost of the option.

**PARTICIPATION RATE** – The percentage of positive index movement credited to the annuity. If the index methodology determined that the index increased 10 percent and the indexed annuity participated in 60 percent of the increase, it would be said that the contract has a 60 percent participation rate. Participation rates may also be expressed as asset fees or yield spreads.

**POINT-TO-POINT** – A crediting method measuring index movement from an absolute initial point to the absolute end point for a period. An index had a period starting value of 100 and a period ending value of 120. A point-to-point method would record a positive index movement of 20 [120-100] or a 20 percent positive movement [(120-100)/100]. Point-to-point usually refers to annual periods; however the phrase is also used instead of term end point to refer to multiple year periods.

**PREMIUM BONUS** – A premium bonus is additional money that is credited to the accumulation account of an annuity policy under certain conditions.

**PUT OPTION** *(ALSO SEE CALL OPTION)* – Gives the holder the right to sell an underlying security or index at a specified price on or before a given date.

**QUALIFIED ANNUITIES** *(QUALIFIED MONEY)* – Qualified annuities are annuities purchased for funding an IRA, 403(b) tax-deferred annuity or other type of retirement arrangements. An IRA or qualified retirement plan provides the tax deferral. An annuity contract should be used to fund an IRA or qualified retirement plan to benefit from an annuity's features other than tax deferral, including the safety features, lifetime income payout option and death benefit protection.

**REQUIRED MINIMUM DISTRIBUTION** *(RMD)* – The amount of money that Traditional, SEP and SIMPLE IRA owners and qualified plan participants must begin distributing from their retirement accounts by April 1 following the year they reach age 70.5. RMD amounts must then be distributed each subsequent year.

**RETURN FLOOR** – Another way of saying minimum guaranteed return.

**ROTH IRA** – Like other IRA accounts, the Roth IRA is simply a holding account that manages your stocks, bonds, annuities, mutual funds and CD's. However, future withdrawals (including earnings and interest) are typically tax-advantaged once the account has been open for five years and the account holder is age 59.5.

**RULE OF 72** – Tells you approximately how many years it takes a sum to double at a given rate. It's handy to be able to figure out, without using a calculator, that when you're earning a 6 percent return, for example, by dividing 6 percent into 72, you'll find that it takes 12 years for money to double. Conversely, if you know it took a sum twelve years to double you could divide 12 into 72 to determine the annual return (6 percent).

**SIMPLE INTEREST** *(ALSO SEE <u>COMPOUND INTEREST)</u>* – Interest is only earned on the principal balance.

**SPLIT ANNUITY** – A split annuity is the term given to an effective strategy that utilizes two or more different annuity products—one designed to generate monthly income and the other to restore the original starting principal over a set period of time.

**STANDARD & POOR'S 500** *(S&P 500)* – The most widely used external index by fixed indexed annuities. Its objective is to be a benchmark to measure and report overall U.S. stock market performance. It includes a representative sample of 500 common stocks from companies trading on the New York Stock Exchange, American Stock Exchange, and NASDAQ National Market System. The index represents the price or market value of the underlying stocks and does not include the value of reinvested dividends of the underlying stocks.

**STOCK MARKET INDEX** – A report created from a type of statistical measurement that shows up or down changes in a specific financial market, usually expressed as points and as a percentage, in a number of related markets, or in an economy as a whole (i.e. S&P 500 or New York Stock Exchange).

**SURRENDER CHARGE** – A charge imposed for withdrawing funds or terminating an annuity contract prematurely. There is no industry standard for surrender charges, that is, each annuity product has its own unique surrender charge schedule. The charge is usually expressed as a percentage of the amount withdrawn prematurely from the contract. The percentage tends to decline over time, ultimately becoming zero.

**TRADITIONAL IRA** – See IRA (Individual Retirement Account)

**TERM END POINT** – Crediting methods measuring index movements over a greater timeframe than a year or two. The opposite of an annual reset method. Also referred to as a term point-to-point method. Say that the index value was at 100 on the first day of the period. If the calculated index value was at 150 at the end of the period the positive index movement would be 50 percent (150-100/100). The company would credit a percentage of this movement as excess interest. Index movement is calculated and interest credited at the end of the term and interim movements during the period are ignored.

**TERM HIGH POINT** *(HIGH WATER MARK)* – A type of term end point structure that uses the highest anniversary index level as the end point. Say that the index value was at 100 on the first day of the period, reached a value of 160 at the end of a contract year during the period, and ended the period at 150. A term high point method would use the 160 value—the highest contract anniversary point reached during the period, as the end point and the gross index gain would be 60 percent (160-100/100). The company would then apply a participation rate to the gain.

**TERM YIELD SPREAD** – A type of term end point structure which calculates the total index gain for a period, computes the annual compound rate of return deducts a yield spread from the annual rate of return and then recalculates the total index gain for the period based on the net annual rate. Say that an index increased from 100 to 200 by the end of a nine year period. This is the equivalent of an 8 percent compound annual interest rate. If the annuity had a 2 percent term yield spread this would be deducted from the annual interest rate (8 percent-2 percent) and the net rate would be credited to the contract (6 percent) for each of the nine years. Total index gain may also be computed by using the highest anniversary index level as the end point.

**VARIABLE ANNUITY** – A contract issued by an insurance company offering separate accounts invested in a wide variety of stocks and/or bonds. The investment risk is borne by the annuity owner. Variable annuities are considered securities and require appropriate securities registration.

**1035 EXCHANGE** – The 1035 exchange refers to the section of tax code that allows annuity owners the flexibility to exchange one annuity for another without incurring any immediate tax liabilities. This action is most often utilized when an annuity holder decides they want to upgrade an annuity to a more favorable one, but they do not want to activate unnecessary tax liabilities that would typically be encountered when surrendering an existing annuity contract.

**401(K) ROLLOVER** – See IRA Rollover

Made in the USA
Lexington, KY
27 June 2017